WORK BOOK 2

キーワードで「現代」を伝える

通訳ワークブック2

浅野輝子／吉見かおる／
グラスプール・ルーシー／ミッシェル・エノー・モローネ 編著

AI and Its Impact on Human Society
人工知能とテクノロジー
Who's watching?
見ているのは誰か？
ポストコロナを生きる
Living in a post-Corona world
平成が生んだポップカルチャー　道徳の在り方を考える
Pop Culture
Lessons from Literature
Politics
ポピュリズムと外交
パンデミックの歴史
Terminology & its history
AIと教育
Education with AI
Literature
国境を超える文学
[ステイホーム]のライフスタイル
"Stay Home": A new mode of daily life
"Work style reform"
働き方改革
What is the university's role? 大学の役割とは何か
ファクトチェック
The rise of misinformation
共同体としての相互援助
Community spirit
橋の架からないところに橋を架ける

NUFS 英語教育シリーズ

名古屋外国語大学出版会
Nagoya University of Foreign Studies Press

まえがき

　名古屋外国語大学では2007年より、各大学の代表学生が対談逐次通訳に挑む、「学生通訳コンテスト」を毎年開催しております。対談では、その年に注目された社会の出来事をテーマに取り上げており、本書「通訳ワークブック2」には2018年、2019年、2020年のスクリプトが収録されています。

　第1のトピック「AIと人間社会に与えるその影響」では、AI技術の発展に対し、人間はどこまで機械に頼ることができるのかを問い、第2のトピック「平成から令和への願い」では平成から令和にかけて起きた出来事を通してその変遷を辿り、第3のトピック「ポストコロナの世界を生きる―パンデミックからの教訓」は、コロナ感染症によって世界はどう変わったかを考察します。これらのトピックは、まさに私たち人間社会のターニングポイントであると言えるでしょう。

　通訳教材は、通訳技術を学べるだけでなく、内容からも知識が得られるものがベストであると考えています。このテキストを使って通訳技術、そして深い教養を身につけていただけることを願っております。

　各トピックの巻頭エッセイは、「学生通訳コンテスト」で審査員をお務めいただいている船山仲他先生、関沢紘一先生、鶴田知佳子先生に、あとがきは、同時通訳デモンストレーションを担当される柴原智幸先生にご執筆いただくことができ、心より感謝申し上げます。

　本書の出版に当たり、貴重なご助言をいただきました、名古屋外国語大学出版会の編集長、大岩昌子先生をはじめ、編集主任の川端博様、出版会の皆様には厚く御礼申し上げます。なお、本書の音声収録にあたり、名古屋学芸大学の森幸長先生にご尽力いただきました。また、名古屋外国語大学非常勤講師の遠藤加奈子先生にもお手伝いいただいたことを申し添えます。

著者代表　浅野輝子

CONTENTS

この本の使い方

① 用語の学習：各サブトピックの Keywords リストより、用語を学ぶ。

② 音声を聞いてシャドーウィング

③ 通訳練習：パラグラフごとに音声を聞きながらメモを取り、メモを元に
通訳する。
見返した時にイメージが浮かぶようなメモを取ることが重要。通訳の際
は、単語の訳にのみ集中せず、「スピーカーの意図は何か」を常に考え
ながら訳すこと。

④ 翻訳練習（復習として）：通訳した内容を再度翻訳し、モデル訳と自分
の訳を比較・修正する（「翻訳分析シート」を使用してください）。

なお、音声・メモ用紙・翻訳分析シートは以下のサイトよりダウンロード
いただけます。

https://nufs-up.jp/download/index.html

TOPIC 1:
AI and Its Impact on Human Society
AI と人間社会に与えるその影響

❶ Introduction: AI and Technology　人工知能とテクノロジー

❷ Medicine and Ethics: How medicine is changing
　　どのように医学は変化を遂げているか

❸ The Arts: How are they affected?　芸術はどのように影響されるか

❹ Politics: AI's impact on the system
　　人工知能が与える政治システムへの影響

❺ Academics: Education with AI　人工知能による教育

❻ Legal Issues: How are they affected?　責任への問い

❼ Economics and Cryptocurrency: Changing people's work lives
　　人間の労働生活における変化

❽ Privacy and Security: Who's watching?　誰が見ているのか

❾ Lessons from Literature　道徳の在り方を考える

❿ Liberal Arts in a Globalized Age: What is the university's role?
　　大学の役割とは何か

■ Simultaneous demonstration
　　AI and humanity　人工知能と人間性

第12回 学生通訳コンテスト スクリプト
2018年11月24日 開催

逐次通訳でも同時通訳でも

船山　仲他
（学生通訳コンテスト審査員長）

　社会一般では、話者交替のある逐次通訳よりも同時通訳の方が難しいという印象があるようです。しかし、昔から、通訳の完成度に関して、"逐次に入って逐次に出る"という言い方もあるように、単純にどっちが難しいという話ではないと考えた方がいいでしょう。ただ通訳のやり方が違うだけのことと捉えた方がいいでしょう。しかし、逐次と同時の違いを考えることには、通訳の本質を捉える点で役立つことがあります。つまり、通訳一般をより本質的に捉えることにつながります。

　通訳をやってみたいと興味を感じる人は、速く"訳語を探す"ことに関心があるでしょう。その視点から逐次通訳と同時通訳の形態を比較すると、同時通訳の方がせかされますから、少なくとも、"修行"としては同時通訳に挑むべきではないか、と思う人もいるかもしれません。あるいは、自分は早口ではないから逐次通訳が向いているのではないか、と考える人がいるかもしれません。しかし、舌の回りの"速さ"よりももっと重要なことがあります。それは、聞き手としての通訳者の"理解の速さ"です。

　では、通訳者にとって"理解"とは何でしょうか。理解の対象となるアイデアはどこにあるのでしょうか。それは、もちろん、原発話者の頭の中にあります。言い換えれば原発話者が言いたいことです。そう捉えると、通翻訳の出発点はその話し手、書き手が言いたいことを理解することにあります。なぜこのことを強調するのか、と言えば、通翻訳の本質が人と人との間のコミュニケーションであることを忘れてはいけないからです。言い換えれば、言語表現の言い換えが自動的に進行することはあり得ません。プロ通訳者がどんどん訳語を出しているように聞こえても、それを支えているのは単に言語表現レベルの作業ではありません。実際には、その通訳者の頭の中では言語表現を支える"思考"がフル回転しているのです。ただ、それをどう自覚するかは別問題と考えた方がいいでしょう。そして、自分でやってみないとその感覚は捉えがたいでしょう。

　こういう"理屈"を理解するためには、とりあえず自分で通訳をしてみることが必要です。逐次でも同時でも本質は同じです。

船山　仲他 / Funayama, Chuta
神戸市外国語大学元学長。現在同大学名誉教授。多数の国際会議で英語－日本語間の同時通訳を担当。1982年大阪外国語大学（現大阪大学外国語学部）で同時通訳演習の授業を始め、大学の通訳教育に従事。通訳理論の研究も進め、日本通訳学会（現日本通訳翻訳学会）設立に参画（理事、会長歴任）。

1

Introduction: AI and Technology

人工知能とテクノロジー

1-0　　Moderator 1

Let's open this topic with some general comments about the impact of technology and AI. Could you each discuss your idea of how technology has developed and found its permanent place in society?

通　訳

1-1　Japanese Speaker 1

はい。目覚ましい発展を続ける AI 技術は、すでに私たちの生活に欠かせないものとなりました。しかし同時に、「AI とは何か」という質問に対して、具体的に答えられる人は限られているかもしれません。AI とは日本語で「人工知能」と訳されます。この用語は、「コンピューター上に人間の知能を再現したもの、またはするための技術」と説明されることが多いです。AI という用語が誕生したのは1956年のことで、ダートマス会議でジョン・マッカーシーによって命名されました。

通　訳

1-2　Japanese Speaker 2

AI と聞くと、ロボットをイメージする人が多いかもしれません。もちろん、自動運転やロボットのように、それ自体が知的な働きをするものを AI と呼ぶことが多いですが、掃除機や炊飯器のように、一見すると単純な動作のみを行っているものにも AI を組み込むことが可能です。AI が開発されてから早60年が経ち、2016年にはアメリカのディープマインド社が開発した囲碁プログラム「アルファ碁」が世界トップレベルのプロ棋士を打ち負かし、脚光を浴びる出来事となりました。

通　訳

1-3　English Speaker 1

Technology is the creation of tools and methods used to achieve an objective. One of the first forms of technology was how our primitive ancestors learned to control fire, eventually creating the sophisticated tools that date from the time of the agricultural revolution. In later periods, human inventions would contribute to the great civilizations of China, Egypt, India, and Mesopotamia. So, intelligence can be described as the ability to solve problems. Artificial intelligence, based on human logic and reason, continues to gain dominance with advances in computer technology. Now, a 'super-intelligent machine' has the potential to self-improve beyond human capabilities.

通　訳

1-4　English Speaker 2

Technological advances have allowed people to live in permanent settlements rather than spending all day long hunting or gathering food. In one place and with more time, work could be shared and ideas improved. Humans began to ponder the abstract, and widen their knowledge of the world. Organized societies had advantages. Social anthropologists believe that good nutrition, economic and political stability, and denser populations are responsible for places with the greatest frequency of idea generation.

通　訳

1-5　Japanese Speaker 3

ドイツ人哲学者であったマルティン・ハイデガーは、著書『技術への問い』の中で、テクノロジーと哲学との関連性について述べています。ハイデガーによれば、そもそも、古代ギリシャにおける「テクネ (techne)」と呼ばれる「技術」は、「アート」である「芸術」をも含めたものであると論じています。つまり、「技術」という用語は、現代的な意味における単なる「道具」に限らず、人間の生命に深くかかわるものであるという解釈です。

通　訳

1-6　English Speaker 3

The theory of the singularity of super intelligence has been proposed by Ray Kurzweil and others. The idea is based on Moore's Law, which discusses technology's development in the digital age. According to the theory, the fast pace of technology will cause human intelligence to grow exponentially. So, we will reach a point where ideas can only be shared in a cloud. This type of intelligence will far surpass what we can imagine now. Opposing this, some argue that ancient humans were far more intelligent biologically and that making mistakes is part of the process of learning, and that sensing the environment in both body and mind is crucial to true human intelligence.

通　訳

1-7　Moderator 2

Thank you very much. You both suggest that the human need to improve society is endless. It follows that the creation of new technologies with AI, for good and for bad, is an inevitable outcome of human curiosity.

通　訳

① Introduction: AI and Technology
人工知能とテクノロジー

欠かせない	indispensable
用語	term
再現	reproduction
ダートマス会議（1956年）	Dartmouth Conference
ジョン・マッカーシー（1927-2011）	John McCarthy
命名する	name
ロボット	robot
組み込む	include
ディープマインド社	DeepMind
囲碁プログラム「アルファ碁」	board game program 'Alpha Go'
プロ棋士	professional Go player
脚光を浴びる	in the spotlight
マルティン・ハイデガー（1889-1976）	Martin Heidegger
『技術への問い』（1954年）	"The Question concerning Technology" (*Die Frage nach der Technik*)
古代ギリシャ	Ancient Greece
「テクネ（*techne*）」	*techne*
現代的な意味	modernistic meaning

methods	手法
objective (n.)	目的
primitive ancestors	祖先
sophisticated	高度な
agricultural revolution	農業革命
civilization	文明
Mesopotamia	メソポタミア
dominance	支配
'super-intelligent machine'	「超知能機械」
ponder	考えを巡らせる
abstract (n.)	抽象
social anthropologist	社会人類学者
generation	生み出す場所
theory of singularity	シンギュラリティの理論
Ray Kurzweil (1948-)	レイ・カーツワイル
Moore's Law	ムーアの法則
digital age	デジタル時代
exponentially	飛躍的に
crucial	重要

1-0   **Moderator 1**

まず、テクノロジーと AI はどのような影響を与えてきたかについて取り上げましょう。お二人には、テクノロジーはどのように進歩しながら、社会の中で確固たる地位を占めるに至ったかについてお話しいただけたらと思います。

1-1   **Japanese Speaker 1**

Certainly. The continued and striking development of AI technology has already made it <u>indispensable</u> to our lives. At the same time, however, there may only be a limited number of people who can give a definite answer to the question "What is AI?" In Japanese, AI is translated as *jinkō chinō*. This <u>term</u> is often explained as "the <u>reproduction</u> of human intelligence by computer, or technology for that purpose." The term AI was coined in 1956, and was <u>named</u> at the <u>Dartmouth Conference</u> by <u>John McCarthy</u>.

1-2   **Japanese Speaker 2**

When hearing 'AI', the image many people may have is of <u>robots</u>. Of course, like automatically operating machines and robots, things that in themselves do intelligent work are often called AI; but it is possible that things like vacuum cleaners and rice cookers, which at first glance perform only simple operations, may also be <u>included</u> in AI. In 2016, 60 years after AI was first developed, the <u>board game program</u> 'Alpha Go' developed by U.S. company <u>DeepMind</u> defeated a world top-ranking <u>professional Go player</u>, an event that put AI <u>in the spotlight</u>.

1-3   **English Speaker 1**

テクノロジーとは、ある<u>目的</u>を果たすために使う道具と<u>手法</u>を生み出すことです。テクノロジーの最初の形は、はるか昔に我々の<u>祖先</u>が習得した火を操る術であり、これによって、<u>農業革命</u>の時代には高度な道具を創り出すようになりました。それから後、人類の発明（の数々）は、中国、エジプト、インド、<u>メソポタミア</u>等の偉大な<u>文明</u>に貢献することになります。つまり、知能とは、問題を解決する能力のことであると説明できます。人工知能は、人間の論理と理性に基づき、コンピューター技術の進歩と共に<u>支配</u>の幅を広げています。今や、「<u>超知能機械</u>」は人間の能力を越え、それ自体が進歩していく可能性を秘めています。

1-4   **English Speaker 2**

テクノロジーの進歩により、人々は狩りや（食料の）採集に 1 日を費やすのではなく、定住して生活することができるようになりました。定まった地で暮らし、時間に余裕が生まれたことで、仕事を分担し、豊かな発想もできるようになりました。人々は抽象的なものに考えを<u>巡らせる</u>ようになり、世界に関する知識を広げ始めました。まとまりのある社会には数々の利点が生まれたのです。<u>社会人類学者</u>たちは、栄養状態が良いこと、経済的・政治的に安定していること、そして人口密度が比較的高めであることが、高い頻度でアイデアを<u>生み出す</u>場所となる要因であると考えています。

1-5　Japanese Speaker 3

German philosopher <u>Martin Heidegger</u>, in his work "<u>The Question concerning Technology</u>", talks about the relationship between technology and philosophy. Heidegger argues that originally, in <u>Ancient Greece</u>, 'technology' or *techne* also included 'art'. In other words, the term 'technology' can be interpreted as not limited to the <u>modernistic meaning</u> of a mere 'tool', but is something that deeply affects human existence.

1-6　English Speaker 3

超知能における<u>シンギュラリティの理論</u>は、<u>レイ・カーツワイル</u>などによって提唱されてきたもので、<u>デジタル時代におけるテクノロジーの発展について論じたムーアの法則</u>に基づいています。この理論よると、テクノロジーの急速な発展により、人間の知能は飛躍的に成長します。つまり、様々な考えがクラウド上でしか共有されない時代が来るということです。この種の知能は、今現在、私たちが想像しているものを遥かに上回ることでしょう。これとは逆に、古代人のほうが生物学的にずっと賢かった、失敗をすることは学習過程の一部である、周囲の環境を心身共に感じとることこそが真の人間の知性にとって最も<u>重要であると主張する人もいます</u>。

1-7　Moderator 2

ありがとうございました。お二人とも、これからも人間は社会をますます良いものにしていく必要があることを語ってくださいました。AI と共に新しいテクノロジーが生み出されているのは、良い意味でも悪い意味でも、人間の飽くなき好奇心の結果ということですね。

2

Medicine and Ethics: How medicine is changing

どのように医学は変化を遂げているか

Keywords

dexterity	疾病検査<ruby>（しっぺい）</ruby>
endurance	精密度
gastrointestinal examination	東京大学医科学研究所
STAR robot	画期的な診療
tip of the iceberg	専門医
nano-world	白血病
genetics	医学論文
medical ethics	担当医
unborn child	医療現場
potential (adj.)	生命倫理
systemic	延命
healthcare system	コンセンサス
caregiver	人の命を預かる
monitor (v.)	補助ツール
	CT
	細胞検査
	顔色
	既往歴
	総合力
	人間力

2-0　Moderator 1

Medical research has improved and extended our lives. Would you comment on the relationship between medicine and technology, and how the introduction of AI is altering medicine?

通　訳

2-1 English Speaker 1

The doctor's role as a skilled professional is changing. For example, a surgeon must have great dexterity, endurance, and knowledge because one is not certain how long and difficult an operation might be. However, now there are robotic aids to assist with many medical procedures. Some may insert an artificial heart valve; others may be used in the cameras for gastrointestinal examinations. The role of AI has become even more dominant in such procedures. In a recent test between a robot and a human, the STAR robot outperformed in a surgery repairing a live pig's severed intestine.

(通 訳)

2-2 English Speaker 2

But this represents only the tip of the iceberg. Aside from the procedures done in the exam room, there is also the nano-world of genetics and medical research. The development of nano-technology challenges medical ethics, especially when knowledge of genetics offers detailed information about the future. For example, should individuals have the right to make decisions about their own health? Is it right for a parent to choose an unborn child's characteristics or for a person to better know the potential reasons for their own death?

(通 訳)

2-3 Japanese Speaker 1

日本でも、AI を活用した癌などの疾病検査、治療方法の提供に関する精密度は、人間の医師を越え始めているとも言われています。2016年、東京大学医科学研究所において画期的な診療が行われました。このケースでは、専門医でも診断が難しいとされる60代の女性患者の特殊な白血病を、約2,000万件の医学論文を学習した AI が10分ほどで見抜き、担当医に適切な治療法をアドバイスしてその女性の命を救ったのです。

(通 訳)

2-4 　Japanese Speaker 2

確かに、AI が医療現場に貢献することが大いに期待されるなか、人間の生命に関わる判断を AI に許してしまうことは、生命倫理の観点から考えると、楽観的に受け入れることはできません。また、AI がいかに正確な情報をつかみ的確な判断を下すことができたとしても、それを患者が信用できるか否かという問題は別の話です。数十年経てば、医療面においても AI を信じたほうがより健康的に延命できるというコンセンサスが社会的に成り立つかもしれません。しかし、現段階では機械の診断結果を患者に適切に伝えられるのは、やはり人間である医者です。

通　訳

2-5 　English Speaker 3

Developments in AI challenge our current ethical, financial, and systemic frameworks. Another AI impact on medicine is how it will affect the healthcare systems that keep track of all the data. Great amounts of patient data will be linked automatically among caregivers, researchers, insurance companies, and the public. How to keep this information safe yet accessible poses a great problem. It is important to create safeguards to ensure that private information is not leaked to the wrong places. Also, who will be responsible for monitoring this valuable public and private store of information?

通　訳

2-6 　Japanese Speaker 3

今では医療現場に AI はなくてはならないものです。同時に人の命を預かるこの分野において、AI はあくまで補助ツールであり、今後も医師が必要とされることに変わりはありません。CT や細胞検査などの結果が正しいかどうかの最終判断や、診察の際の患者の顔色や受け答えのスピード、また既往歴、職業など、様々な要素を組み合わせて診断するのは医師です。AI は記憶、また計算することは得意ですが、総合力、創造性、コミュニケーション能力は人間にしか備わっていません。そのため、医師には人間力がより一層必要とされることは言うまでもありません。

通　訳

2-7 　Moderator 2

AI has encouraged change very quickly. Improvements in medicine involve ethical questions that will continue to challenge humans in the future. Thank you for your comments.

通　訳

② Medicine and Ethics: How medicine is changing
どのように医学は変化を遂げているか

dexterity	器用さ
endurance	持久力
gastrointestinal examination	消化管検査
STAR robot	STAR ロボット
tip of the iceberg	氷山の一角
nano-world	ナノの世界
genetics	遺伝学
medical ethics	医学倫理
unborn child	生まれてくる子ども
potential (adj.)	なり得る
systemic	組織的な
healthcare system	医療制度
caregiver	介護士
monitor (v.)	監視する

疾病検査 (しっぺい)	examinations for diseases
精密度	precision
東京大学医科学研究所	University of Tokyo Institute of Medical Science
画期的な診療	ground-breaking diagnosis and treatment
専門医	medical specialists
白血病	leukemia
医学論文	medical articles
担当医	attending physician
医療現場	medical treatment setting
生命倫理	bioethics
延命	prolong one's life
コンセンサス	consensus
人の命を預かる	responsibility for human life
補助ツール	auxiliary tool
CT	CT (Computed Tomography)
細胞検査	cytodiagnosis
顔色	complexion
既往歴	case history
総合力	comprehension
人間力	human qualities

2-0   Moderator 1

医学の研究が進歩し、私たちの寿命が延びました。医学とテクノロジーはどのように関わっているのか、また、AI の導入により医療現場はどのように変わったのか、お話しいただけますか。

2-1   English Speaker 1

特殊技能を備え持つ専門家としての医師の役割は変化しています。例えば、外科医は優れた手先の器用さや、持久力、そして知識を持っている必要があります。なぜなら手術にどれくらい時間がかかり、どれほど難しいものになるのか確信が持てないからです。しかし、今では、多くの医療処置を補助する支援ロボットがあります。人工心臓弁を挿入するロボットもあるかもしれませんし、消化管検査に使用されるカメラに使われているかもしれません。このような医療処置において人工知能の役割はよりいっそう広がってきています。最近行われたロボットと人間のテストでは、STAR ロボットの方が生きた豚の切断された腸を修復する手術で、人間よりも優れた結果を残しました。

2-2   English Speaker 2

しかし、これは氷山の一角に過ぎません。診察室で行われる処置の他にも、遺伝学や医学研究といったナノの世界もあります。特に遺伝学の知識が、将来に関する詳しい情報を提示する際に、ナノテクノロジーの開発は医学倫理に挑むことになります。例えば、個人は自分の健康について決める権利を持つべきでしょうか。親が生まれてくる子どもの特徴を選んだり、また個人が自身の死因となり得るものについて知ったりすることは良いのでしょうか。

2-3   Japanese Speaker 1

In Japan, also, it is said that the precision of AI being used in examinations for diseases like cancer, and in the provision of therapeutic strategies, is starting to go beyond human doctors. In 2016 ground-breaking diagnosis and treatment was carried out at the University of Tokyo Institute of Medical Science. In this case, an AI that had studied 20 million medical articles was able to detect an unusual form of leukemia, which was difficult for medical specialists to diagnose, in a 60-year-old female patient; the AI gave advice on appropriate treatment to the attending physician, and the woman's life was saved.

2-4　Japanese Speaker 2

Certainly, within the high hopes of the contribution AI will make in a medical treatment setting, if we think from the perspective of bioethics the idea of AI being permitted to make judgements regarding human life cannot be accepted optimistically. Further, however accurate the information and appropriate the conclusions drawn by the AI might be, whether the patient will be able to trust them is a different question. After several decades we may as a society reach the consensus that trusting AI in the medical field can healthily prolong our lives. However, at the current stage the ones who can appropriately convey the results of machine diagnosis to patients are of course human physicians.

2-5　English Speaker 3

人工知能の発展は、現代の私たちが持つ倫理的、金銭的、組織的な骨組みに課題を提示するものです。また、医学におけるもう一つの人工知能の影響は、全てのデータを記録する医療制度にどのように作用するかということです。膨大な量の患者情報は介護士、研究者、保険会社、一般の人々の間で自動的に共有されるでしょう。この情報をいかに安全で、なおかつアクセスしやすい状態にしておくかが大きな課題となります。個人情報を間違ったところに流出させないように、確実な対策を立てることが重要です。それでは、こういった一連の貴重な公私に及ぶ情報を監視するとなると、いったい誰が責任を負うのでしょうか。

2-6　Japanese Speaker 3

In the field of medical care, AI is now something we cannot do without. At the same time, in the area of responsibility for human life, AI is simply an auxiliary tool, and doctors will continue to be essential. The doctor makes the final judgement on whether the results of a CT or cytodiagnosis are correct, and makes a diagnosis based on a combination of various factors such as the patient's complexion and response speed during the examination, as well as their case history, occupation, etc. AI's forte is memory and calculation; but comprehension, creativity, and communication ability are only possessed by humans. Hence it goes without saying that, for doctors, human qualities are even more important.

2-7　Moderator 2

AIは急速な変化を促してきました。医療の発展と共に、今後も倫理的な問題が出てきますね。ご意見ありがとうございました。

The Arts:
How are they affected?

芸術はどのように影響されるか

3-0　Moderator 1

AI is already used in many areas of leisure and art. Can you discuss some of the noticeable changes in the arts now and the implications for the future?

通 訳

3-1 **Japanese Speaker 1**

はい。「芸術（アート）」という用語の意味を調べると、芸術は極めて人間的な活動であることがわかります。しかし、この分野においても近年 AI の応用が始まり、様々な議論がなされています。それは他でもなく、「AI から生まれる作品は芸術作品と言えるのか」という議論です。その代表的な例は、2016年にアメリカのマイクロソフト社が大学や美術館と共同で実施したプロジェクト「The Next Rembrandt」です。このプロジェクトでは、AI を使用して17世紀のオランダ人画家・レンブラントの「新作」を作るというものでした。

通 訳

3-2 **Japanese Speaker 2**

音楽の分野における AI の開発は、グーグルが行っているプロジェクト「Magenta」があります。機械学習を用いて優れたアートや音楽を生み出せるかどうかを試すこのプロジェクトでは、AI が作ったピアノ曲が公開されています。最近では、音楽サービス「A.I. Duet」も発表されており、画面に表示される鍵盤でメロディーを奏でると、それに合わせたようなメロディーを AI が返してくれるという仕組みです。日本でも、ヤマハの AI がダンサーの動きを音楽表現に変換する「ダンス認識ピアノ演奏システム」の開発に成功しました。

通 訳

3-3 **English Speaker 1**

Yes, as AI collaborates more with the art world, there is more interest in reexamining the contributions and techniques of great artists of the past. The virtual aspect of art may affect the quality and quantity of how art is created, performed, and even how it is perceived. Using technology, some researchers are examining the place in the brain where art is experienced. They are investigating how sensory manipulation affects the way the brain processes information at the synapse level.

通 訳

3-4　English Speaker 2

It seems natural for creators like those in the art and music world today to rely heavily on AI technology. Yet we must not forget that throughout the ages, art and music have always welcomed technological advances. Today, AI in interactive art can be witnessed in the installations of Maurice Benayoun or Jeffrey Shaw, where spectators become the 'visitors' experiencing the works. The perception of the artistic creation depends on the interaction between the visitor and the AI-generated art piece. This challenges a fixed, traditional idea of what aesthetics is.

通　訳

3-5　Japanese Speaker 3

このように、芸術の分野でも AI に関する数々の先進的な試みがなされています。しかし、人間が備え持つ果てしない創造力に比べ、このような蓄積されたデータから生まれる作品により、AI は「創造力を獲得した」と言えるのでしょうか。原理上、AI に大量のデータを読み込ませ、「美しいもの」と「美しくないもの」を教えれば、いずれ美の概念を獲得することでしょう。しかし、イタリアのルネッサンス期に活躍したミケランジェロや、ロシアのチャイコフスキーなどが人類に残した芸術の遺産を考えると、真の芸術作品はどのようなものであるか、誰もが理解することができると思います。

通　訳

3-6　English Speaker 3

When an artist creates a piece, it is believed that he or she owns it. A price, a monetary value, is associated with it. But a recent movement in the art world rejects this tradition. With AI, creativity has become something to be shared, and is not the property of one creator. An artistic concept begins. Responders look at the product and add to it. They may even change the initial idea completely. The art product is an ongoing expression. So, if art is the product of a community, where does creativity exist and how do we reward it?

通　訳

3-7　Moderator 2

Thank you for your commentaries. As AI becomes part of the arts, our concept of what art and leisure are may change in ways that may make them difficult to recognize in the future.

通　訳

❸ The Arts: How are they affected?
芸術はどのように影響されるか

マイクロソフト社	Microsoft
プロジェクト「The Next Rembrandt」	project 'The Next Rembrandt'
レンブラント（1606-1669）	Rembrandt Harmenszoon van Rijn
グーグル	Google
「Magenta」	'Magenta'
機械学習	machine learning
「A.I. Duet」	'A.I. Duet'
鍵盤	keyboard
メロディーを奏でる	play a melody
「ダンス認識ピアノ演奏システム」	'Dance Recognition Piano Performance System'
先進的な試み	advanced experiment
果てしない	boundless
創造力を獲得する	acquire creativity
概念	general idea
ルネッサンス期	Renaissance
ミケランジェロ（1475-1564）	Michelangelo di Lodovico Buonarroti Simoni
チャイコフスキー（1840-1893）	Peter Ilyich Tchaikovsky
芸術の遺産	artistic legacy

perceive	捉える
manipulation	操作
synapse	シナプス
technological advances	技術的な進歩
Maurice Benayoun (1957-)	モーリス・ベナユン
Jeffrey Shaw (1944-)	ジェフリー・ショウ
spectator	鑑賞者
generate	生み出す
aesthetics	美学
monetary value	金銭的価値
movement in the art world	芸術界の動き
creativity	創造性
ongoing	常に〜し続ける

③-0　Moderator 1

AI は、娯楽や芸術の様々な場面ですでに使用されています。現在の芸術における顕著な変化と未来への影響についてお話しいただけますか。

③-1　Japanese Speaker 1

Yes. If we investigate the meaning of the term 'art', we find that the arts are a very human activity. However, in recent years the application of AI has begun in this field too, leading to various disputes. The discussion here is: "Can a work born from AI be called a work of art?" An exemplary instance of this is the project 'The Next Rembrandt', which was implemented in collaboration between the U.S. company Microsoft, universities, and art galleries. This project used AI to create a 'new work' by the 17th century Dutch painter Rembrandt.

③-2　Japanese Speaker 2

For development of AI in the field of music there is project 'Magenta', carried out by Google. This project, which is testing whether outstanding art and music can be created using machine learning, has publicly released a piano composition created by AI. Recently a music service, 'A.I. Duet', has been presented; this is a mechanism in which, if you play a melody on the keyboard displayed on the screen, the AI will play a complementary melody back to you. In Japan too, the development of Yamaha's 'Dance Recognition Piano Performance System', in which AI converts a dancer's movements into musical representation, has been a hit.

③-3　English Speaker 1

そうですね。AI が芸術の世界とコラボレーションを進めるにつれて、過去の偉大な芸術家たちの貢献や技術の再調査への関心が高まります。芸術のバーチャルな側面が、芸術の創造や表現に質的、量的に影響を与えることもあり、また受け手の捉え方にも影響をもたらす可能性があります。テクノロジーを使用して芸術を感知する脳の部位を研究している者もいます。シナプスレベルでの脳の情報処理方法に、感覚の操作がどのように影響を及ぼすかを調査しています。

③-4　English Speaker 2

今日の芸術や音楽の世界に身を置くクリエイターたちが AI テクノロジーに大きく依存するのは当然のことであるように思えます。しかし、芸術と音楽は時代を通して、常に技術的な進歩を受け入れてきたことを忘れてはいけません。今日、AI は双方向的芸術の中で、モーリス・ベナユンやジェフリー・ショウのインスタレーション作品に見られますが、そこでは鑑賞者はその作品を体験する「訪問者」となります。その訪問者と AI が生み出す芸術作品の相互の交流によって、芸術作品の感じ方は決まります。これは、「美学とは何か」という伝統的な考え方に疑問を投げかけるものです。

3-5   Japanese Speaker 3

In this way, even the arts field is seeing many <u>advanced experiments</u> in AI. However, in comparison with the <u>boundless</u> creativity possessed by humans, can we say AI has '<u>acquired creativity</u>' through of works born from an accumulation of data? In principle, if AI is allowed to read massive amounts of data and we can teach it what is 'beautiful' and 'not beautiful', it may acquire a <u>general idea</u> of beauty. However, if we think of the <u>artistic legacies</u> left to humanity by the likes of <u>Michelangelo</u>, who played an active role during the Italian <u>Renaissance</u>, or Russia's <u>Tchaikovsky</u>, I think that what makes a true work of art can be understood by everyone.

3-6   English Speaker 3

芸術家が作品を作るとき、芸術家自身がその作品を所有すると考えられます。そこには値段、つまり<u>金銭的価値</u>が付随します。しかし、近頃の<u>芸術界の動き</u>はこの伝統を否定しています。AIを伴うことで、<u>創造性</u>は共有されるものとなり、1人の芸術家の所有物ではなくなります。ここからが芸術的概念の始まりです。受け手側はその作品を見ると同時に創造性を加えていきます。なので、当初の考えが完全に変わってしまうこともあり得ます。芸術作品は<u>常に変化し続ける</u>表現となっていきます。したがって、もし芸術がコミュニティの物であるなら、その創造性は誰のもので、それに対する金銭的価値はどうなるのでしょうか。

3-7   Moderator 2

お話しいただきありがとうございました。AIが芸術の一部となったことで、私たちのもつ芸術や娯楽の概念は変化し、将来的に認識しづらくなる可能性があるのですね。

4

Politics:
AI's impact on the system
人工知能が与える政治システムへの影響

Keywords	
liberal democracy	トランプ政権
informed public	フェイク・ニュース
cripple (v.)	初代ローマ皇帝アウグストゥス
Donald Trump (1946-)	アントニウス（83 B.D.-30 B.D.）
bring to light	中傷する
pose (v.)	流通する
free form	故意に
streaming	悪用
propaganda	政治参加
fake news	チュニジア
target (v.)	「ジャスミン革命」（2011年）
profile (v.)	汚職
influence voters	反政府デモ
division within society	統治する
populist movement	ベン・アリ政権（期間：1987-2011年）
borderless	転覆する
ISIS	飛び火する
social networks	オックスフォード英字辞書
breeding ground	「ポスト真実」
AI systems	客観的な事実
manipulate	個人的信条
public opinion	曖昧さ
address (v.)	蔓延する
pose a threat	健全な批評力
witness (v.)	判別する
bots	
influence voting	
Trump election	
Brexit discussion	
Emmanuel Macron (1977-)	
undermine	

4-0 ▐ **Moderator 1**

The politics of an era tell us what is valued at the time. Can you begin the discussion of how AI has affected events in the political sphere?

(通 訳)

4-1 ▐ **English Speaker 1**

Yes. Liberal democracy requires an informed public. Without this, its function is crippled. In 2016, the election of Donald Trump brought to light the threat the Internet poses to media information. Without regulations or the proper confirmation of information sources, the Internet allows free form streaming of propaganda and fake news. The AI used on the Internet can target like-minded people and profile them. In this way it is easy to influence voters. Division within society results, which has contributed to the increase of populist movements worldwide.

(通 訳)

4-2 ▐ **English Speaker 2**

In this borderless Internet world, groups like ISIS were able to use social network platforms to recruit supporters from around the world. A social network platform like Facebook, for example, was originally created with good intentions. But now it can be used as a breeding ground for unintended use. Sharing responsibility for this, Facebook, Twitter, Google, and Microsoft have already teamed together to work on AI systems that can better detect terrorist propaganda.

(通 訳)

4-3 ▐ **Japanese Speaker 1**

トランプ政権が発足してから、「フェイク・ニュース」という言葉を頻繁に耳にするようになりました。しかし、これは真新しい現象ではありません。その歴史を遡ると、紀元前、初代ローマ皇帝アウグストゥスが、敵であるアントニウスを中傷するコインを流通させたというエピソードがあります。まさにその行為は、政治的影響力を狙ったものでした。フェイク・ニュースとは、その名の通り「偽りのニュース」を意味します。「政治目的やウェブサイトへのアクセスを促すため、サイトから故意に配信される偽情報や作り話」と定義されています。

(通 訳)

4-4　Japanese Speaker 2

ソーシャルメディアの政治的な<u>悪用</u>が存在する一方で、若者の<u>政治参加</u>を可能にさせた出来事も同時に忘れてはなりません。2011年に<u>チュニジア</u>で起こった「<u>ジャスミン革命</u>」は、まさにその例です。当時、貧困と警察の<u>汚職</u>に苦しむ若者が自らの命を絶ったことがフェイスブックで拡散されたことをきっかけに、そこから大きな<u>反政府デモ</u>が起こりました。その結果、長期にわたりチュニジアを<u>統治</u>してきたベン・アリ政権が<u>転覆</u>します。これをきっかけに、政治的な目的を達成しようと、一般市民がソーシャルメディアを利用してデモを行う動きが世界中に<u>飛び火</u>しました。

［　通　訳　］

4-5　English Speaker 3

How AI is able to <u>manipulate</u> <u>public opinion</u> is the first step to <u>addressing</u> how it <u>poses a threat</u> to democratic political systems. We have <u>witnessed</u> how computer- generated <u>bots</u> were used to encourage emotions; they <u>influenced</u> <u>voting</u> in the cases of the US <u>Trump election</u>, the UK <u>Brexit discussions</u>, and the leaking of false information about <u>Macron</u>. Such examples <u>undermine</u> public trust in government.

［　通　訳　］

4-6　Japanese Speaker 3

2016年の「今年の言葉」として、<u>オックスフォード英字辞書</u>は「<u>ポスト真実</u>」を選びました。その定義は、「世論を形成する際に、<u>客観的な事実</u>よりも、むしろ感情や<u>個人的信条</u>へのアピールの方がより影響力があるような状況」とされています。つまり、現代は、真実が重要でも適切でもなくなった時期にさしかかっているということです。情報の<u>曖昧さが蔓延する</u>なかで、私たちは特に政治に関わる情報に対して<u>健全な批評力</u>を養わなければなりません。なぜなら、AI には読解力が備わっていないため、フェイク・ニュースを<u>判別する</u>ことはできないからです。

［　通　訳　］

4-7　Moderator 2

As you suggest, politics and media are very much linked today. We must be very careful what and how we read when choosing who to vote for.

［　通　訳　］

④ Politics: AI's impact on the system
人工知能が与える政治システムへの影響

liberal democracy	自由民主主義
informed public	情報に通じた国民
cripple (v.)	果たせない
Donald Trump (1946-)	ドナルド・トランプ
bring to light	明らかになる
pose (v.)	及ぼす
free form	様々な形
streaming	絶え間なく流される
propaganda	プロパガンダ
fake news	フェイクニュース
target (v.)	対象とする
profile (v.)	記録する
influence voters	投票者に影響を与える
division within society	社会の分裂
populist movement	大衆主義運動
borderless	境界線のない
ISIS	ISIS
social networks	ソーシャルネットワーク
breeding ground	温床
AI systems	人工知能システム
manipulate	操作する
public opinion	世論
address (v.)	伝える
pose a threat	脅かす
witness (v.)	目の当たりにする
bots	ボット
influence voting	投票に影響を与える
Trump election	トランプ大統領が選出された選挙
Brexit discussion	EU 離脱問題
Emmanuel Macron (1977-)	マクロン大統領
undermine	弱体化させる

トランプ政権	Trump administration
フェイク・ニュース	fake news
初代ローマ皇帝アウグストゥス	first Roman emperor, Augustus Caesar (63 B.C.-14 A.D.)
アントニウス（83 B.D.-30 B.D.)	Marcus Antonius
中傷する	libel (v.)
流通する	distributed
故意に	in bad faith
悪用	misuse (n.)
政治参加	political participation
チュニジア	Tunisia
「ジャスミン革命」（2011年)	'Jasmine Revolution'
汚職	corruption
反政府デモ	antigovernment demonstrations
統治する	rule (v.)
ベン・アリ政権（期間：1987-2011年)	Ben Ali administration
転覆する	be overthrown
飛び火する	be sparked
オックスフォード英字辞書	Oxford English Dictionary
「ポスト真実」	'post-truth'
客観的な事実	objective truth
個人的信条	personal convictions
曖昧さ	ambiguity
蔓延する	spread (v.)
健全な批評力	healthy power of criticism
判別する	distinguish

4-0　Moderator 1

政治の在り方は、その時代の価値観を表しています。政治的な出来事に AI がどの様に影響してきたのか、お話しいただけますでしょうか。

4-1　English Speaker 1

はい。自由民主主義は情報に通じた国民を必要とします。これが欠けると、その機能は果たせません。2016年のドナルド・トランプが選出された大統領選挙で、インターネットがメディア情報に及ぼす脅威が明らかになりました。規制や情報源の適切な確認が無ければ、インターネットにより実に様々な形で、プロパガンダやフェイクニュースが絶え間なく流されてしまいます。インターネットで利用される人工知能は、同じ考えを持つ人々を対象とし、その人物像を記録します。このように、投票者に影響を与えることは容易いことです。社会の分裂が生じた結果、世界中の大衆主義運動が高まりを見せているのです。

4-2　English Speaker 2

この境界線のないインターネットの世界では、ISIS のような組織が世界中から支援者を募るためにソーシャルネットワーク上のプラットフォームを利用することができました。例えばフェイスブックのようなソーシャルネットワーク上のプラットフォームは、本来、前向きな意図を持ってつくられました。しかし今では、その目的から外れた様々な利用のされ方をする温床となっています。フェイスブック、ツイッター、グーグル、そしてマイクロソフトはこの責任を共有し、すでにチームを組んでテロリストのプロパガンダを見抜くより高性能な人工知能システムの開発に取り掛かっています。

4-3　Japanese Speaker 1

Since the inauguration of the Trump administration, we have come to hear the words 'fake news' incessantly. However, this is not a brand-new phenomenon. If we go back in history, in the pre-Christian era the first Roman emperor, Augustus Caesar, distributed coins libeling his rival, Antonius. This conduct was almost certainly aimed at gaining political influence. Fake news, as the name suggests, means 'fabricated news'. It is defined as "disinformation or fabricated stories distributed in bad faith by websites, either with a political aim or to stimulate access to a website."

4-4　Japanese Speaker 2

While political misuse of social media exists, at the same time we must not forget the examples of how it has enabled young people's political participation. The 2011 'Jasmine Revolution' that occurred in Tunisia is certainly an example of this. At the time, young people suffering under poverty and police corruption spread the fact of their own suppression on Facebook, causing large antigovernment demonstrations. As a result, the Ben Ali administration, which had ruled Tunisia for a long period, was overthrown. Inspired by this, demo activities by the general public using social media were sparked across the world.

4-5　English Speaker 3

人工知能がどのように世論操作できるかという点が、民主的な政治体制を脅かすことを伝えるための最初のキーポイントとなるのです。私たちはコンピューターで作ったボットがどのように感情を助長するのに使われたかを目の当たりにしてきました。それらはトランプ大統領が選出されたアメリカの大統領選挙における投票や、イギリスのEU離脱問題、そしてマクロン大統領に関する誤った情報の漏洩に影響を与えたのです。先に述べたような出来事は政府に対する国民の信頼を弱体化させます。

4-6　Japanese Speaker 3

In 2016 the Oxford English Dictionary chose 'post-truth' as its 'Word of the Year'. The definition is "a state of affairs in which appeals to emotion and personal convictions are more influential than objective truth in forming public opinion". In short, we are now on the verge of a time in which truth, however important and relevant, has disappeared. Within the spread of the ambiguity of information we must maintain a healthy power of criticism, especially of information connected to politics. This is because AI is not furnished with the ability to read and understand, and therefore cannot distinguish fake news.

4-7　Moderator 2

ご指摘のとおり、政治とメディアは今日強く結びついています。だれに投票するかを決める際には、何をどのように読むべきか、気をつけなければいけませんね。

5

Academics:
Education with AI

人工知能による教育

Keywords

「東ロボくん」	imbedded
国立情報学研究所	pedagogy
全国センター模擬試験	proponent
知識量	administrative tasks
読解力	checking attendance
物事の意義	assessment
存在価値	interactive teaching
意識を深める	ability to concentrate
被造物	score (n.)
教育の根幹	imply
「フィロソフィア (*philosophia*)」	subconscious expectation
「ソフィア (*sophia*)」である「智」	retrieve
「愛する (*philia*)」	discern
「エドゥコ (*educo*)」	erroneous
内在する	Internet addiction
AI ロボット「ペッパー」	rehab camp (rehabilitation camp)
幼児教育	
教育の課程	
昆虫採取	
生き生きとした	

5-0　　**Moderator 1**

Education and technology have come a long way since the digital age. Would you start the discussion with your comments on AI's role in education?

通　訳

5 -1　Japanese Speaker 1

はい。皆さんは「東ロボくん」をご存知でしょうか。このロボットは、2011年から国立情報学研究所などが人工知能の可能性を探るために取り組んだプロジェクトです。実際に2016年、全国センター模擬試験に挑んだ結果、受験生の平均をかなり上回りました。科目別にみると、成績がよかったのは数学や物理、そして知識量がものをいう世界史などです。一方で、国語や英語は伸び悩み、その原因としてこのAIロボットには「読解力」がないという問題が指摘されました。

(通　訳)

5 -2　Japanese Speaker 2

人間とは、物事の意義を常に問いかけ、また成長を重ねるにつれて自己の存在価値に対しても意識を深めていく被造物です。これこそ哲学の根本であり、教育の根幹を成すものです。事実、哲学の語源はギリシャ語の「フィロソフィア（*philosophia*）」に由来し、「ソフィア（*sophia*）」である「智」を「愛する（*philia*）」という意味です。では、「教育」の意味はどうでしょうか。教育 'education' の語源はラテン語で「エドゥコ（*educo*）」と言い、「既に内在するものを外に引き出す」という意味があります。

(通　訳)

5 -3　English Speaker 1

Technology in the classroom is nothing new. However, the increasing use of AI imbedded in basic educational pedagogy questions the continuing role of the teacher to both instruct and guide in the traditional way. The proponents of AI argue it lessens the administrative tasks like checking attendance, assignments, giving feedback and assessments, which allows time for the teacher to research more creative teaching, to monitor the AI system, and to spend time on more interactive teaching with the students.

(通　訳)

5-4 English Speaker 2

Research has shown the effects of AI on the <u>ability to concentrate</u>. In an experiment done on college students performing a simple math test, all students were asked to turn off their cell phones. One group took their phones into the test and the other group left their phones outside. The test results for the group without their phones showed a 15% higher <u>score</u>. This <u>implies</u> that a <u>subconscious expectation</u> to check the cell phone, even turned off, affects the ability to concentrate.

(通 訳)

5-5 Japanese Speaker 3

近年、日本国内のいくつかの幼稚園で、<u>AIロボット「ペッパー」</u>を導入した<u>幼児教育</u>が始まりました。このロボットは、友だちまた教師の代わりとなり、子どもたちとコミュニケーションを取ると言います。<u>教育の過程</u>で最も重要な課題は、学びの喜びを子どもに教えることです。例えば、ある先生が授業のなかで<u>昆虫採取</u>の話をするとします。その話を聞く生徒は、昆虫に関する知識を学び、その先生の<u>生き生きとした</u>経験をも共有することができます。このような経験の共有は、人の心を育てる上で非常に重要な要素であり、AIにはできないことです。

(通 訳)

5-6 English Speaker 3

With AI, worldwide resources are limitless and easily <u>retrieved</u>, so a greater need to teach people how to <u>discern</u> good information from the <u>erroneous</u> is crucial, as well as a focus on self-control in the increasingly AI world. We are already witnessing how this might affect the internal motivation of young students, both physically and mentally. Research done in China indicated that those afflicted with severe <u>Internet addiction</u> show an 8% decrease in brain function along with other physical ailments, prompting the creation of <u>rehab camps</u> in the country.

(通 訳)

5-7 Moderator 2

Thank you for elaborating on this topic, professors. Surely, more research is necessary to investigate more concretely how AI helps or hinders learning for the individual and what kind of students we are preparing for society.

(通 訳)

Academics: Education with AI
人工知能による教育

「東ロボくん」	'Tōrobo-kun'
国立情報学研究所	National Institute of Informatics
全国センター模擬試験	mock national Center Examination
知識量	level of knowledge
読解力	reading comprehension ability
物事の意義	meaning of things
存在価値	raison d'être
意識を深める	deepen significance
被造物	creature
教育の根幹	foundation of education
「フィロソフィア（*philosophia*）」	*philosophia*
「ソフィア（*sophia*）」である「智」	'wisdom (*sophia*)'
「愛する（*philia*）」	'love of (*philia*)'
「エドゥコ（*educo*）」	*educo*
内在する	have inside
AIロボット「ペッパー」	AI robot 'Pepper'
幼児教育	preschool education
教育の課程	education process
昆虫採取	bug collecting
生き生きとした	vivid
imbedded	組み込まれる
pedagogy	教授法
proponent	支持者
administrative tasks	事務的な作業
checking attendance	出欠確認
assessment	評価
interactive teaching	双方向的な授業
ability to concentrate	集中力
score (n.)	点数
imply	暗示する
subconscious expectation	潜在意識
retrieve	入手する
discern	区別する
erroneous	間違った
Internet addiction	インターネット中毒
rehab camp (rehabilitation camp)	リハビリ施設

5-0   Moderator 1

教育とテクノロジーはデジタル時代に入ってから長い道のりを経ています。まず、AI の教育における役割についてのご意見からお話しを進めていただけますか。

5-1   Japanese Speaker 1

Certainly. Perhaps you all know 'Tōrobo-kun'? This robot is a project by the National Institute of Informatics and others who have been investigating the possibilities of Artificial Intelligence since 2011. Actually, the results of a mock national Center Examination in 2016 showed that it did rather better than the average student score. If we take it by subject, the robot got good grades in Mathematics and Physics, and its level of knowledge came in handy in World History, etc. On the other hand it didn't do so well in Japanese or English; the cause is this AI robot's lack of reading comprehension ability, a problem that was pointed out.

5-2   Japanese Speaker 2

Humans are creatures who are constantly questioning the meaning of things, and, as we continue to develop, the significance of our own raison d'être deepens. This is at the root of philosophy, and forms the foundation of education. In fact the etymology of philosophy comes from the Greek word *philosophia*, which means the 'love of (*philia*)' 'wisdom (*sophia*)'. So what is the meaning of 'education'? The etymology of 'education' is said to be from the Latin word *educo*, which means "to draw out the things we already have inside us".

5-3   English Speaker 1

教室内でテクノロジーを用いることは珍しいことではありません。しかしながら、基本的な教授法に組み込まれる人工知能利用の増加は、従来の教師の役割、つまり伝統的な方法で知識を与え、規範を示すという「指導」に疑問を投げかけています。人工知能の支持者たちは、人工知能の利用により教師の出欠確認や課題、フィードバック、評価といった事務的な作業にかかる時間が減り、創造的な教育の探求や、人工知能システムの管理、生徒との双方向的な授業に多くの時間を割くことができると主張しています。

5-4   English Speaker 2

人工知能が集中力に与える影響が調査により明らかになりました。簡単な数学の試験を受ける大学生に対して行われた実験では、すべての学生が携帯電話の電源を切ることを求められました。一方の集団は携帯電話を試験室に持ち込み、もう一方の集団は携帯電話を試験室に持ち込みませんでした。その試験結果では、携帯電話を持ち込まなかった集団の方が15%点数が高いということが示されました。携帯電話の電源が入っていなくても、携帯電話を確認したいという潜在意識が働き、集中力に影響を与えるということを暗示しています。

5 -5 　Japanese Speaker 3

Recently, preschool education began introducing an AI robot 'Pepper' into a number of kindergartens around Japan. It's said that this robot will communicate with the children as a proxy for friends and teachers. However, the most important task of the education process is to teach children the pleasure of learning. For example, in class a teacher is talking about bug collecting. The listening students can learn information about insects and even share the teacher's vivid experience. Sharing such experiences is a vital component of educating a person's heart and mind, and is something that cannot be done by AI.

5 -6 　English Speaker 3

人工知能によって、世界中の情報を無限に、且つ容易に入手することができるため、正しい情報と間違った情報を区別する力を養う必要があり、人工知能が急速に普及する世界において自制心を保つことも重要となります。若い学生たちの内なるやる気に、心身共に影響を及ぼすことがすでにわかってきています。中国で行われた調査結果によると、深刻なインターネット中毒に苦しむ人は、体の病気に加えて8%脳機能が低下していることが明らかになり、中国国内では、早急にリハビリ施設の建設が促されています。

5 -7 　Moderator 2

先生方、このトピックについて語っていただきありがとうございました。まだこれからAIが個人の学習に役立つのか、妨げになるのかを探り、どんな学生を社会に送り出すかについても議論を進める必要がありますね。

6

Legal Issues: How are they affected?

責任への問い

Keywords

image processing	「ディープラーニング」
algorithm	革新的
facial recognition	想定外
outside sources	取り締まる
potential (n.)	知能化した
legal world	「電子人間」
determination of responsibility	法的地位を付与する
driverless car	白熱する
legal expert	欧州議会
liability system	自律型ロボット
tax	決議案
compensation	自動運転車
taxed fund	自律的な判断を行う
system of credits	責任範囲
Mercedes	企業家
passenger	公開書簡
injury	思考プロセス
legal changes	「ブラックボックス問題」
individual's right to privacy	社会的議論
accusation	法的概念
Facebook CEO, Mark Zuckerberg (1984-)	メーカー
leak (v.)	責任の所在
Cambridge Analytica	絡み合う
highlight (v.)	ハッキング
	包括的な議論

6-0 Moderator 1

Problems can be anticipated with the rise of automated AI systems utilized in our society. Can you discuss some of the legal issues that may arise with AI?

（ 通 訳 ）

6-1 English Speaker 1

One example is in the area of image processing, which uses algorithms to analyze an image used in facial recognition. It automatically determines the health of a person and his or her location. It can verify a piece of handwriting. Such a system that learns automatically from outside sources has the potential to act in ways its creators could not have predicted. And when it happens that AI systems act independently, where does responsibility lie? This is the overall worry regarding AI in the legal world.

（ 通 訳 ）

6-2 English Speaker 2

Legal issues deal with the determination of responsibility. In the case where a driverless car is involved in an accident, who is to blame? Some legal experts in the EU suggest a new liability system be created: driverless cars will be taxed. Should there be an accident, compensation is paid from this taxed fund. In China, some suggest a system of credits that shows a car owner's law-abiding record can be used. Another idea suggested by the Mercedes company gives its car owners and passengers priority over disputes in an injury case.

（ 通 訳 ）

6-3 Japanese Speaker 1

AI には、人間に指示を出されなくてもそれ自体で考えを発展させることも可能です。その力を「ディープラーニング」と呼び、とても革新的である一方、人間の手を離れた所で想定外の行動を起こす可能性もあります。では、AI が他人に損害を与えてしまったとしたら、誰が責任を取ればいいのでしょうか。AI 自体は機械であるため、人の行為を規制するために作られた現在の法律では取り締まることができないのが現状です。ですが近年、AI の発展によって知能化したロボットに、「電子人間」といった新しい概念の法的地位を付与することが望ましいか否かの議論が国際舞台で白熱し始めています。

（ 通 訳 ）

6-4 Japanese Speaker 2

2017年2月、欧州議会は、自ら学習する機能を持った自律型ロボットに対して、「電子人間」を人として扱えるように法的地位を与えるべきだとの決議案を通過させました。自動運転車のような自律的な判断を行う AI ロボットが相次いで登場しているため、被害発生時の責任範囲を明確にする必要があったからです。これに対し、欧州連合14カ国の AI の専門家、弁護士、そして企業家156名が、欧州委員会に公開書簡を送り、「電子人間」の概念の導入に強く反対しました。

通 訳

6-5 English Speaker 3

Yet AI develops faster than legal changes can occur. Other legal issues regard an individual's right to privacy. One example is the accusations faced by Facebook CEO, Mark Zuckerberg. He admitted that Facebook had allowed personal information to be leaked to Cambridge Analytica, which then used the information to influence the 2016 US election campaign. His apology in court for the problem highlights how AI mechanisms occur beyond human control.

通 訳

6-6 Japanese Speaker 3

現在、高度な自律型ロボットはまだ登場していません。しかし、AI の思考プロセスを人間が把握することができないという「ブラックボックス問題」のリスクがあるため、前もって社会的議論と法的概念を整える必要があります。現在、自動運転車などが起こした事故は、メーカーと被害者間の個別交渉で処理されています。しかし将来的に、メーカー、所有者、オペレータなど、責任の所在が複雑に絡み合った事故が起きたり、ハッキングやネットワーク事故など特定の企業が責任を負いきれない可能性が生じたりするなど、充分考えられます。今後も、包括的な議論が必要とされるでしょう。

通 訳

6-7 Moderator 2

Thank you for illuminating some of the legal challenges we will face as AI becomes more a part of society's institutions. It is certain to change the legal field as we know it now.

通 訳

⑥ Legal Issues: How are they affected?
責任への問い

image processing	画像処理
algorithm	アルゴリズム
facial recognition	顔認証
outside sources	外部の情報源
potential (n.)	可能性
legal world	法律面
determination of responsibility	責任の所在を決定する
driverless car	無人自動車
legal expert	法律の専門家
liability system	賠償責任制度
tax	課税する
compensation	賠償金
taxed fund	税金
system of credits	債務制度
Mercedes	メルセデスベンツ
passenger	同乗者
injury	傷害
legal changes	法改正
individual's right to privacy	個人のプライバシー権
accusation	告発
Facebook CEO, Mark Zuckerberg (1984-)	フェイスブック最高経営責任者・マーク・ザッカーバーグ
leak (v.)	漏洩する
Cambridge Analytica	ケンブリッジ・アナリティカ
highlight (v.)	浮き彫りにする

「ディープラーニング」	'deep learning'
革新的	innovative
想定外	unforeseen
取り締まる	be regulated
知能化した	become intelligent
「電子人間」	'electronic personhood'
法的地位を付与する	conferring legal status
白熱する	heat (v.)
欧州議会	European Parliament
自律型ロボット	autonomous robot
決議案	resolution
自動運転車	self-driving car
自律的な判断を行う	make autonomous decision
責任範囲	area of responsibility
企業家	entrepreneur
公開書簡	open letter
思考プロセス	thought process
「ブラックボックス問題」	'black box problem'
社会的議論	social debates
法的概念	legal concept
メーカー	manufacturer
責任の所在	site of responsibility
絡み合う	be tangled
ハッキング	hacking
包括的な議論	comprehensive discussion

6-0 Moderator 1

AI が社会に浸透するにつれて問題も出てくると思われますが、特に法律面での問題点についてお話しいただけますか。

6-1 English Speaker 1

一つの例は画像処理の分野にありますが、そこでは顔認証で使われている画像を解析するためにアルゴリズムを用います。それは自動的に人の健康状態や位置を特定します。筆跡の一部分を使用して照合が可能です。外部の情報源から自動的に学習するそういったシステムは創作者が予想だにしなかった行動を起こす可能性があります。そして人工知能システムが勝手に動くとき、その責任の所在はどこになるのでしょうか。この点が AI の法律面での懸念材料となります。

6-2 English Speaker 2

法的な問題として、責任の所在を決定することもあります。無人自動車が事故に遭遇した場合、誰が責任を負うのでしょうか。欧州連合の法律の専門家たちは、新しい賠償責任制度を創り上げるべきだと提案しています。無人自動車も課税対象になり、万一事故があった場合、賠償金はこの税金から支払われます。中国では、車の持ち主の順法記録を示す債務制度も使えると提案する人たちがいます。その他、メルセデスベンツ社からの提案としては、傷害事件で争った場合、自社の車の所有者と同乗者に優先権が与えられるとしています。

6-3 Japanese Speaker 1

Even if not instructed by humans, AI has the potential to develop its own thought. This ability is called 'deep learning' and, while highly innovative, it can cause unforeseen behavior independent of humans. So, if AI causes harm to another person, who should assume responsibility? Because AI itself is a machine, under today's laws, which were created in order to govern human behavior, AI cannot currently be regulated. However, in recent years heated debates have begun on the international stage regarding the desirability of conferring legal status on a new concept known as 'electronic personhood' for robots that have become intelligent through the development of AI.

6-4　Japanese Speaker 2

In February 2017, the European Parliament passed a resolution that autonomous robots with the ability to self-learn should be treated as people and given the legal status 'electronic human'. This was because AI robots such as self-driving cars, which make autonomous decisions, are successively being introduced into the market; therefore it is necessary to define the area of responsibility whenever harm is caused. In contrast, AI experts from 14 European Union countries, plus lawyers and 156 entrepreneurs, sent an open letter to the European Commission in which they strongly opposed the introduction of the 'electronic human' concept.

6-5　English Speaker 3

しかし人工知能は法改正がなされる以上の速さで発展しています。その他の法的問題は個人のプライバシー権に関しての問題です。一つの例として、フェイスブックの最高経営責任者であるマーク・ザッカーバーグが直面した告発があります。彼はフェイスブックがケンブリッジ・アナリティカ社に個人情報を漏洩させたことを認めましたが、その会社はそれからその情報を使用して2016年のアメリカ大統領選に影響を与えました。この問題に対する彼の法廷での謝罪は、人工知能の仕組みがいかに人間の制御を上回るものかということを浮き彫りにしました。

6-6　Japanese Speaker 3

Currently, no sophisticated autonomous robots have been introduced on the market. However, because of the risk of the 'black box problem', in which AI's thought processes cannot be grasped by humans, it is necessary to prepare social debates and legal concepts in advance. Right now accidents caused by self-driving cars and the like are dealt with through individual negotiation between the manufacturer and the injured party. However, we can imagine many future examples: accidents will occur in which the site of responsibility becomes complicated and tangled among the manufacturer, owner, and operator, etc.; or hacking or network accidents may occur in which a specific company cannot take full responsibility. From now on it will be essential to hold comprehensive discussions about this.

6-7　Moderator 2

AIが社会に浸透するにつれ、法的な問題点があちらこちらで出てくることが示されました。確実に法律分野も今とは変わるでしょう。

Economics and Cryptocurrency: Changing people's work lives

人間の労働生活における変化

Keywords

革命的	siphon off
デジタル通貨	algorithmic
「ビットコイン」	digital dictatorship
紙幣	comradeship
硬貨	(become) obsolete
仮想通貨	oppression
元年	policy makers
投資対象	ultimate
日本銀行	irrelevant
「ブロックチェーン」	
取引履歴	
担保される	
取引所	
破綻する	
補償する	
人を介さない	
「技術的失業」	
経済学用語	
オックスフォード大学	
マイケル・オズボーン（1982-)	
カール・ベネディクト・フレイ	
『雇用の未来』	
論文	
消滅する	

7-0　Moderator 1

Economics is also a field that will change with the increasing use of AI working its systems. Can you begin this topic with your impression of cryptocurrency and its effects?

通 訳

7-1　Japanese Speaker 1

はい。現在、全世界で使用することのできる革命的なデジタル通貨として、「ビットコイン」が大いに注目を集めています。仮想通貨とは、その名の通りバーチャルな通貨なので、紙幣や硬貨といった形が存在しません。自分が保有するコインの額や、また使用した額など、すべてのデータはインターネット上で管理されます。さらに、スマートフォン一つで、いつでも、世界中の誰にでも、個人間で自由に送金することができる通貨です。昨年2017年は、仮想通貨元年と呼ばれました。

通 訳

7-2　Japanese Speaker 2

投資対象として注目されている「ビットコイン」ですが、メリットだけではなく、デメリットもしっかりと把握する必要があります。仮想通貨は、日本銀行などが発行する「円」とは異なる通貨であるため、特定の管理者は存在せず、「ブロックチェーン」という技術を通して取引履歴を利用者同士が管理します。つまり、国による価値の担保がありません。そのため、「ビットコイン」の場合、取引所が破綻したとしても、国によって補償されることはありません。

通 訳

7-3　English Speaker 1

Yes, the growing presence of cryptocurrency makes us aware that social and economic crises must be addressed. We give up security by allowing our devices to do everything for us. We allow our information to be siphoned off to automatic algorithmic systems. In doing so, AI creates a kind of digital dictatorship. It controls voting in politics and allows us to lose control of our money. Also, it will make many jobs done by humans unnecessary. It is estimated that within 30 years, fifty percent of jobs will have been eliminated with this new form of economy.

通 訳

7-4 English Speaker 2

In the present-day world, individuals obtain meaning from work. As social animals, humans feel comradeship by working with others. But a combination of the revolutions occurring in information technology and bio-technology will render many types of jobs obsolete. More and more services will be done automatically by AI. At the same time, the physical lives of humans will be extended for years with little work to do.

通 訳

7-5 Japanese Speaker 3

AI の発達により、人を介さないで経済が成り立っていくことも可能になった現在、「技術的失業」という新たな問題が懸念されています。「技術的失業」とは経済学用語で、「新しい技術の導入がもたらす失業」を意味しています。オックスフォード大学のマイケル・オズボーンとカール・ベネディクト・フレイは2013年、『雇用の未来』という論文のなかで、今後20年以内には、アメリカの総雇用者の約47%の仕事がコンピューターにとって代わられ消滅する、と述べています。消滅する仕事の数は、実に700の職種に上っています。

通 訳

7-6 English Speaker 3

Oppression will not come from the government and policy makers. Instead, a handful of elite, skilled experts will have ultimate control in combination with AI. Most of the population, however, will have little to do. To address the potential reality of billions of people seeing their lives as irrelevant, new jobs will have to be created that focus on things AI cannot do; in particular caring skills or a focus on greater mindfulness.

通 訳

7-7 Moderator 2

So AI makes it possible to automatically trade a currency that is invisible. Thank you for discussing the potential consequences of such a system.

通 訳

7 Economics and Cryptocurrency: Changing people's work lives
人間の労働生活における変化

革命的	revolutionary
デジタル通貨	digital currency
「ビットコイン」	'Bitcoin'
紙幣	banknote
硬貨	coin
仮想通貨	cryptocurrency
元年	first year
投資対象	target for investment
日本銀行	the Bank of Japan
「ブロックチェーン」	'Blockchain'
取引履歴	transaction history
担保される	be guaranteed
取引所	stock exchange
破綻する	collapse (v.)
補償する	offer reparations
人を介さない	unmediated by humans
「技術的失業」	'technological unemployment'
経済学用語	economics term
オックスフォード大学	University of Oxford
マイケル・オズボーン（1982-）	Michael Osborne
カール・ベネディクト・フレイ	Carl Benedikt Frey
『雇用の未来』	"The Future of Employment"
論文	article
消滅する	vanish
siphon off	吸い上げる
algorithmic	アルゴリズムの
digital dictatorship	デジタル独裁主義
comradeship	仲間意識
(become) obsolete	廃れる
oppression	抑えつけ
policy makers	政治家
ultimate	とてつもない
irrelevant	無意味なもの

7-0　Moderator 1

経済の分野も AI の職場での使用が増えるにつれ変わってきますね。仮想通貨とその影響についてお考えをお聞かせください。

7-1　Japanese Speaker 1

Of course. Currently, 'Bitcoin' is gaining considerable attention as a revolutionary digital currency that can be used worldwide. Virtual currency, as the name suggests, is virtual money, so it does not exist in the form of banknotes or coins. The amount of 'coins' you own and spend, etc. is managed online entirely in data form. Furthermore, with this currency you can freely send money between individuals, at any time to anyone anywhere in the world, using only a smartphone. Last year, 2017, has been called cryptocurrency's first year.

7-2　Japanese Speaker 2

However, it is necessary to clearly grasp the fact that 'Bitcoin', which has been drawing attention as a target for investment, does not only present advantages but also drawbacks. Because cryptocurrency is a different currency from the 'yen' issued by the Bank of Japan, etc., it has no designated manager: the transaction history is managed mutually by users using a technology known as 'Blockchain'. In other words, its value is not guaranteed by the country. Therefore, even if there is a collapse on the stock exchange the country will not offer reparations.

7-3　English Speaker 1

はい、仮想通貨の広がりにより、私たちは対処しなければならない社会的、経済的な危機感が出てくることに気付かされます。いろいろな機器が私たちに関する全てを担うことで、私たちの安心・安全は失われます。私達自身の情報は自動アルゴリズムシステムに吸い上げられます。そうすることで、人工知能は一種のデジタル独裁主義を創り出します。AI によって、政治における投票は操作され、私たちは自分のお金をコントロールできなくなります。また、人間によって行われている多くの仕事も不要になってしまうでしょう。この新しい経済形態の下で、30年以内に現在ある仕事の内50% の仕事が無くなってしまうと推定されます。

7-4　English Speaker 2

現在の世界では、個、個人は仕事から何らかの意義を得ています。社会的な動物として、人間は他人と働くことで仲間意識を感じます。しかし情報技術分野と生物学的技術分野に起っている変化の数々により、これから多くの職業が廃れていきます。サービス分野は益々人工知能によって自動化されるでしょう。同時に、人間はほとんど仕事をする必要がなくなり、肉体的な寿命はますます伸びていくでしょう。

7-5　Japanese Speaker 3

At this time, in which the viability of economics <u>unmediated by humans</u> has become possible due to the development of AI, an anxiety over '<u>technological unemployment</u>' is becoming a new problem. 'Technological unemployment' is an <u>economics term</u> meaning "unemployment brought about by the introduction of new technology". In a 2013 <u>article</u> titled <u>"The Future of Employment"</u>, by <u>Michael Osborne</u> and <u>Karl Benedikt Frey</u> from the <u>University of Oxford</u>, it is stated that within 20 years the work of 47% of American employers will <u>vanish</u>, replaced by computers. Approximately 700 types of occupation will disappear.

7-6　English Speaker 3

政府や<u>政治家</u>による<u>抑えつけ</u>には見舞われないでしょう。代わりに、一握りのエリートや特殊技能を持つ人たちが人工知能を駆使して<u>とてつもない支配力</u>を持つようになるでしょう。しかしながら、国民の大部分は、ほとんどすることがなくなってしまいます。数十億人の人々が人生を<u>無意味な</u>ものだと見なす恐れがある現実に対処するためには、人工知能には出来ないことに焦点を当てた新しい仕事を創造する必要がありますが、とりわけ人を思いやる技術や卓越した心配りや気遣いができる仕事を創り上げることです。

7-7　Moderator 2

AI により、自動的に目に見えない通貨を使って取引をすることが可能になっています。そのようなシステムの行く末について、お話しいただきありがとうございました。

8

Privacy and Security: Who's watching?

誰が見ているのか

Keywords

ingrain	行政組織
positively correlate	操作する
exploit	飛躍的に
poison (v.)	有権者である国民
cybersecurity	「知る権利」
leak (v.)	情報格差
data deception technology	実態
trick (v.)	浮かび上がる
bots	エドワード・スノーデン（1983-）
GDPR (The General Data Protection Regulation)	告発
	内部告発
export of personal data	議論が高まる
	国連人権理事会
	プライバシー権
	宣言する
	人格を発達させる権利
	基本権
	根幹
	日本国憲法
	明示する
	第13条
	幸福の追求の権利
	条文
	充実した議論

8-0 Moderator 1

The mention of the word AI automatically brings up the issue of security. How can we keep information safe in this dynamic IT world? Could you give your thoughts on this subject please?

通　訳

8-1 English Speaker 1

Yes. AI has quickly become ingrained in our daily lives. This is positively correlated to the amount of personal information we willingly contribute. Without realizing it, choices we make, both private and commercial, are being used. They are translated into computer code algorithms. These stereotype us and predict our motives. Such systems have the potential to be easily exploited or poisoned.

通　訳

8-2 English Speaker 2

Individuals and organizations have information that is useful to others. Cybersecurity aims to protect information from being leaked, as well as to target potential hackers from invading a system. Data deception technology detects, examines, and defends against potential dangers. It can even trick hackers away. Even so, the rapid progress of AI means security must be constantly updated.

通　訳

8-3 Japanese Speaker 1

AIや情報テクノロジーの進化によって、私たちの生活が便利になり、豊かにもなっていますが、同時に個人情報が監視される危険性があることを忘れてはなりません。近年、国家や行政組織、また企業が持つ私たちを監視する能力、また情報収集能力、さらには操作能力が飛躍的に高まっています。しかしその一方で、有権者である国民の「知る権利」、そして責任を問う力が弱まっているのも事実です。

通　訳

8-4　Japanese Speaker 2

現在、国家と国民の間の情報格差は急速に広がっています。この情報格差の実態をくっきりと浮かび上がらせたのが、2013年6月、エドワード・スノーデンによる告発でした。この告発により、政府によって、自国民だけではなく世界中の人々のメールや通話が集められていたことが明らかになりました。これにより、内部告発の重要性、また情報収集能力を高めている国家や行政組織に対して、どのような規制が必要なのかといった議論が高まり、世界中にその衝撃を与えたのです。

通 訳

8-5　English Speaker 3

Because hackers and advanced bots utilize AI, the need for progressively complicated systems of security has escalated. In May 2018, the EU put into effect the General Data Protection Regulation, or GDPR, an EU law that protects the privacy of individuals in the EU. It also restricts the export of personal data even outside the European Union.

通 訳

8-6　Japanese Speaker 3

幸いなことに2017年、国連人権理事会は初めて、プライバシー権が人格の発達を可能にする権利として機能していることを宣言しました。人格を発達させる権利は、あらゆる基本権の根幹です。この権利については日本国憲法に明示されていませんが、第13条に触れられています。そこには、生命、自由、そして幸福の追求の権利の保障が明記されています。今後、自由に人格を発達させる権利をこの条文と結び付けて、より充実した議論が必要となってくるでしょう。

通 訳

8-7　Moderator 2

The world must be prepared for arriving security concerns as AI advances. Your discussion has encouraged greater awareness of what to expect in the coming years.

通 訳

⑧ Privacy and Security: Who's watching?
誰が見ているのか

ingrain	浸透する
positively correlate	強く関わる
exploit	利用する
poison (v.)	弊害となる
cybersecurity	サイバーセキュリティ
leak (v.)	漏洩する
data deception technology	データ偽装工作技術
trick (v.)	だます
bots	ボット
GDPR (The General Data Protection Regulation)	個人情報を保護する法律
export of personal data	個人情報の流出

行政組織	administrative organization
操作する	manipulate
飛躍的に	rapidly
有権者である国民	rights-bearing citizen
「知る権利」	'right to know'
情報格差	information gap
実態	reality
浮かび上がる	bring to life
エドワード・スノーデン（1983-)	Edward Snowden
告発	indictment
内部告発	whistleblowing
議論が高まる	raise discussion
国連人権理事会	United Nations Human Rights Commission
プライバシー権	right to privacy
宣言する	announce
人格を発達させる権利	right to allow the development of individuality
基本権	fundamental human right
根幹	foundation
日本国憲法	The Japanese constitution
明示する	explicitly specify
第13条	Article 13
幸福の追求の権利	right to pursue happiness
条文	provision
充実した議論	substantial discussions

8-0　Moderator 1

AIと聞くと、当然セキュリティーの問題が浮かびますね。このITの巨大な世界で情報を安全に保つにはどうしたら良いのでしょうか。この問題についてお考えを述べていただきますか。

8-1　English Speaker 1

はい。人工知能は私たちの日常生活に急速に浸透してきています。これは私たちが前向きに提供しようとする個人情報量と強く関わっています。気付かない間に、私たちの行う私的な選択や商業的な選択は利用されています。それらの情報はコンピューター記号のアルゴリズムに変換されます。私たちは型にはめられ、私たちの行動を促す選択を予測します。こういったシステムは簡単に不当に利用されたり、弊害となったりする可能性があります。

8-2　English Speaker 2

個人や組織は他人に役立つ情報を持っています。サイバーセキュリティはシステムに侵入する可能性のあるハッカーを標的にすると同時に情報漏洩の防止を目的としています。データ偽装工作技術を使い、潜在的な危険を見抜き、分析し、そして防御します。それはハッカーたちをだまし返すことさえできます。そうだとしても、人工知能が急速に進化していくなかで、セキュリティー面も絶えず更新していかなければなりません。

8-3　Japanese Speaker 1

Through the progress of AI and information technology our lives have become convenient and rich; but we must not forget that at the same time there is a danger of our personal information being monitored. In recent years the ability of nations, administrative organizations, and companies to monitor us, collect our personal information, and manipulate us has been rising rapidly. At the same time, it's a fact that the 'right to know' of rights-bearing citizens and their power to take responsibility for themselves is weakening.

8-4　Japanese Speaker 2

Currently the information gap between nation and citizens is widening rapidly. What clearly brought the reality of this information gap to life was the indictment of Edward Snowden in June 2013. This indictment made it clear that governments have been collecting the emails and phone calls not only of their own country's citizens but also from people around the world. This incident caused worldwide shock, demonstrating the importance of whistleblowing and raising discussion about what kinds of regulations are required regarding the increasing information-gathering powers of nations and administrative organizations.

8-5　English Speaker 3

ハッカーたちや高機能ボットが人工知能を利用するため、更に複雑なセキュリティーシステムの必要性が増しています。2018年5月、欧州連合は一般データ保護規則、GDPRとも言われる欧州連合における個人情報を保護する法律を制定しました。それはまた欧州連合外での個人情報の流出も規制しています。

8-6　Japanese Speaker 3

Fortunately, in 2017 the United Nations Human Rights Commission announced that it was putting the right to privacy into operation as a right that makes the development of individuality possible. The right to allow the development of individuality is the foundation of every fundamental human right. The Japanese constitution does not explicitly specify this right, but it is touched on in Article 13. This clearly specifies the right to pursue life, freedom, and happiness. From now on it will be necessary to combine this provision with the right to freely allow the development of individuality, and to have more substantial discussions.

8-7　Moderator 2

人工知能が進化するにつれて、世界はセキュリティー上の問題にも準備しなければなりません。お二人の話から、これから先、何が起こるかについて大きな関心を持たねばならないことがわかりました。

9

Lessons from Literature

道徳の在り方を考える

Keywords

無用の長物	inherent
中等教育	Greek tragedies
国語	Aesop's fables
夏目漱石（1867-1916）	Penthesilea
芥川龍之介（1892-1927）	Achilles
断片的	Troy
文学を味わう	"The Tortoise and the Hare"
ヨシフ・ブロツキー（1940-1996）	the self
ノーベル文学賞	ponder
ソビエト連邦（ソ連）	food for thought
亡命する	metaphor
市民権	rhythm
教鞭を取る	mirror (v.)
ノーベル賞受賞記念講演	characters
不健全	imperfection
政治綱領	
不幸	
トルストイ（1828-1910）	
名言	
シェイクスピア（1564-1616）	
ダンテ（1265-1321）	
ドストエフスキー（1821-1881）	
世界の文豪	
鮮明に描写される	
心に響く	
共感する	
問いかける	

9-0　Moderator 1

As we discuss the human role in technology, perhaps lessons from literature are valid. Can you give us your thoughts on this?

(通　訳)

9-1　Japanese Speaker 1

はい。現代のグローバル化した世界にあり、文学を学ぶ意義はどのように捉えられているでしょうか。多くの人々は、「文学のような学問は、この時代にあって役に立たない無用の長物だ」と考えるかもしれません。はたして本当にそうなのでしょうか。日本では、文学に触れられる機会はおそらく中等教育の場であり、国語という科目の中で学びます。その中で、日本の作家であれば夏目漱石や芥川龍之介などの作品を扱いますが、断片的に読み進めるため、それでは文学を味わったということにはなりません。

(通　訳)

9-2　Japanese Speaker 2

1987年、ヨシフ・ブロツキーというロシア人の詩人がノーベル文学賞を受賞しました。1972年にソ連からアメリカに亡命し、後にアメリカの市民権を得ていくつもの大学で教鞭を取りました。ブロツキーは、ノーベル賞受賞記念講演の中でこのように語っています。「文学が社会において少数派の財産でしかないという現状は、不健全で危険なことのように思われる。もし我々が社会のリーダーを選ぶときに、候補者の政治綱領ではなく、彼らの読書体験を選択の基準にしたならば、この地上の不幸はもっと少なくなるだろう」と。

(通　訳)

9-3　English Speaker 1

If the lessons inherent in the Greek tragedies or Aesop's fables were of no importance, they could not have lasted. One is reminded that human pain and complexity is nothing new. For example, in the story when Penthesilea fights Achilles at Troy and Achilles kills her, at the moment of her death he falls in love with her. Another example of the universal nature of classic stories is in Aesop's fable of "the Tortoise and the Hare". This story has been so easily adopted into so many cultures that most think of it as their own.

(通　訳)

9 -4　English Speaker 2

The best literature expresses the complexity of the human experience beyond the limits of <u>the self</u>. It takes one beyond one's own generation. The reader as an active participant <u>ponders</u> difficult questions via characters and situations previously unimagined. Such difficulties experienced beyond one's self become the <u>food for thought</u> that can be used throughout one's life. Also, the symbols, <u>metaphors</u>, <u>rhythms</u> and sounds that move the story along <u>mirror</u> what our mind, body, and soul is experiencing.

通　訳

9 -5　Japanese Speaker 3

かつて、<u>トルストイ</u>は「文学はパンのようなもの、科学は水のようなもの」という<u>名言</u>を残しました。つまり、文学は人間が<u>生きる上で</u>なくてはならないものだということです。<u>シェイクスピア</u>、<u>ダンテ</u>、そして<u>ドストエフスキー</u>などが<u>世界の文豪</u>と呼ばれるその理由は、彼らの作品のなかに、人間の苦しみ、痛み、またそこから生まれる希望が<u>鮮明に描写され</u>ているため、それが世界中の読者の<u>心に深く響き</u>、<u>共感され</u>、生きる意義を<u>問いかけ</u>させるからです。

通　訳

9 -6　English Speaker 3

Life lessons are not simple. Two people reading a piece of literature may not interpret it the same. They often come away from a book with completely different feelings about the <u>characters</u> or situations. A reader may even interpret something as a symbol or metaphor that was unintended by the author. But this does not mean it is a mistake. Rather it suggests that <u>imperfection</u> exists in literature just as it does in human life.

通　訳

9 -7　Moderator 2

Thank you very much. It seems that we still have many lessons to re-learn from literature, both past and present.

通　訳

⑨ Lessons from Literature
道徳の在り方を考える

無用の長物	useless
中等教育	secondary education
国語	Japanese Language
夏目漱石（1867-1916）	Natsume Sōseki
芥川龍之介（1892-1927）	Akutagawa Ryūnosuke
断片的	fragmentary
文学を味わう	savor literature
ヨシフ・ブロツキー（1940-1996）	Joseph Brodsky
ノーベル文学賞	Nobel Prize for Literature
ソビエト連邦（ソ連）	Soviet Union
亡命する	seek asylum
市民権	citizenship
教鞭を取る	teach
ノーベル賞受賞記念講演	Nobel Laureate commemorative speech
不健全	unhealthy
政治綱領	political program
不幸	grief
トルストイ（1828-1910）	Ru-Lev Nikolayevich Tolstoy
名言	famous saying
シェイクスピア（1564-1616）	William Shakespeare
ダンテ（1265-1321）	Dante Alighieri
ドストエフスキー（1821-1881）	Fyodor Mikhailovich Dostoevsky
世界の文豪	renowned literary masters
鮮明に描写される	vividly depict
心に響く	move the heart
共感する	feel sympathy
問いかける	interrogate

inherent	（物語などに）出てくる
Greek tragedies	ギリシャ悲劇
Aesop's fables	イソップ童話
Penthesilea	ペンテシレイア
Achilles	アキレウス
Troy	トロイア
"The Tortoise and the Hare"	『うさぎとかめ』
the self	自身の
ponder	深く考える
food for thought	思考の糧
metaphor	隠喩
rhythm	韻
mirror (v.)	反映する
characters	登場人物
imperfection	不完全なもの

9-0　Moderator 1

テクノロジーにおける人間の役割について語るには、文学から学ぶのも大切でしょう。この点について、お考えをお聞かせください。

9-1　Japanese Speaker 1

Yes. In today's globalized world, how are we grasping the significance of studying literature? Perhaps many people think that "disciplines like literature are unhelpful and useless in this day and age". Is that really the case? In Japan, the place where we have the chance to come into contact with literature is perhaps secondary education: it is studied in a class called Japanese Language. It covers the works of Japanese authors such as Natsume Sōseki and Akutagawa Ryūnosuke; but as they are read in a fragmentary way, this is not exactly savoring literature.

9-2　Japanese Speaker 2

In 1987 a Russian poet called Joseph Brodsky was awarded the Nobel Prize for Literature. In 1972 he fled the Soviet Union to seek asylum in the U.S.A.; later he obtained American citizenship and taught in many universities. In his Nobel Laureate commemorative speech, Brodsky said the following: "The condition of society in which literature is the property or prerogative of a minority appears to me unhealthy and dangerous. Had we been choosing our leaders on the basis of the candidates' reading experience and not their political programs, there would be much less grief on earth."*

*Paraphrased from Brodsky's Nobel Lecture, September 8, 1987.

9-3　English Speaker 1

もしギリシャ悲劇やイソップ童話に出てくる教訓が重要でないならば、それらは語り継がれていなかったでしょう。気付かされるのは、人間の苦悩や複雑さというのは今に始まったものではないということです。例えば、ペンテシレイアがアキレウスとトロイアで闘い、アキレウスが彼女を殺した時の物語の中で、彼は彼女が死ぬ瞬間に恋に落ちました。中世の物語に共通する性質のもう一つの例は、イソップ童話の『うさぎとかめ』にあります。この話は多くの文化に受け入れられやすく、皆が自分の国の物語だと思っていました。

9-4　English Speaker 2

最も優れた文学は人間の経験の複雑さを、自身の経験を超えて表現します。世代の枠を超えて、読者をいざないます。物語に入り込んだ読者は、登場人物や想像だにしなかった場面を通し、難しい問題点を深く考えます。自身の経験を超えた難しい問題を思考することは、これから先の人生に有益な糧となります。また、文学の中の象徴、隠喩、韻、そして響きは、私たちの心、体、魂が経験していることを鏡のように反映させながら物語は進行していくのです。

9-5   Japanese Speaker 3

<u>Tolstoy</u>'s <u>famous saying</u> remains with us: "Literature is like bread, science is like water." In other words, literature is something essential to our lives as humans. Why are <u>Shakespeare</u>, <u>Dante</u>, <u>Dostoyevsky</u> and so on called <u>renowned literary masters</u>? Because their works <u>vividly depict</u> human suffering, pain, and the desire born from these things; and so they <u>move the hearts</u> of readers around the world, make them <u>feel sympathy</u>, and cause them to <u>interrogate</u> the meaning of life.

9-6   English Speaker 3

人生の教訓とは単純なものではありません。2人が同じ文学作品を読んでも、解釈が異なるかも知れません。<u>登場人物</u>や状況について全く異なる感情を抱くこともよくあります。著者さえも意図しなかったことを、読者が何かの象徴や隠喩だと解釈することもあり得るのです。しかしこれは決して間違いではなく、むしろ文学も人生と同じように<u>不完全なものである</u>ことを示唆しています。

9-7   Moderator 2

どうもありがとうございました。過去・現在ともに、文学から学びなおすことがまだあるようですね。

10

Liberal Arts in a Globalized Age: What is the university's role?

大学の役割とは何か

Keywords

academia	危機に瀕す
consequences	文部科学省
skepticism	大学設置基準
defend	緩和される
complexity	教養課程
recurring	激減する
mimic (v.)	AI 化
'deep learning'	切っても切れない関係
logical	養う
trial and error	言葉の起源
multitude of perspectives	ギリシア・ローマ
solid liberal arts education	理念的な源流
Albert Einstein (1879-1955)	中世
practical education	技芸
broad-based education	根本的
	亀山郁夫学長（名古屋外国語大学）
	「エンパシー」
	共感する能力
	急速な進展
	不安を抱く
	行動の指針
	振り返る
	糧
	生命力

10-0 Moderator 1

For our next topic, what do you think the role of the university liberal arts is in this technologically dominated world?

(通 訳)

10-1 English Speaker 1

Advances in technology and AI have helped <u>academia</u> to progress exponentially during this century. This progress comes with <u>consequences</u>, even for social institutions like academia. This has increased <u>skepticism</u> about the purposes of a liberal arts curriculum. Universities must <u>defend</u> liberal arts and its benefits. A good student knows themself well, and understands the <u>complexities</u> of human experiences. This student will become a citizen able to think critically.

(通 訳)

10-2 English Speaker 2

The <u>recurring</u> problem of perfecting AI is that it still <u>mimics</u> human intelligence using a mathematical method called '<u>deep learning</u>', which is based on logic. But humans are not always <u>logical</u>. Rather, we are able to solve problems by mistake or by <u>trial and error</u>. AI cannot. In this global age which offers a <u>multitude of perspectives</u>, it is unwise to ignore this. There is hidden value in the wide knowledge gained from a <u>solid liberal arts education</u>.

(通 訳)

10-3 Japanese Speaker 1

日本の大学における教養教育は、現在、<u>危機に瀕している</u>ように思われます。一つには1990年代初頭に、<u>文部科学省</u>の方針によって、<u>大学設置基準</u>が<u>緩和された</u>ことが挙げられます。その結果、大学における<u>教養課程</u>が<u>激減</u>してしまいました。しかし、グローバリゼーション、また<u>AI化</u>という現代に生きる私たちにとって、<u>切っても切れない</u>関係にあるのは、やはり教養です。その教養を<u>養える</u>場所がまさに大学なのです。

(通 訳)

10-4 | **Japanese Speaker 2**

「リベラルアーツ」という言葉の起源は、ギリシア・ローマに理念的な源流を持っています。ヨーロッパの大学制度で中世以降、自由な人間の持つべき技芸の基本と見なされていました。現代の教養課程の在り方にとって、根本的に大事なことは、他者への想像力を養うことです。これは、ここ名古屋外国語大学の亀山学長が「エンパシー」という言葉で表現されるものです。つまり教養とは、他者に共感する能力を養うものと言い換えられます。

(通 訳)

10-5 | **English Speaker 3**

Albert Einstein said: "The value of an education in a liberal arts college is not the learning of many facts but the training of the mind to think". If liberal arts education becomes unpopular in favor of more practical education, the student loses something essential. A broad-based education will help students make informed choices so they can better address the many complexities they will meet in the near future.

(通 訳)

10-6 | **Japanese Speaker 3**

今後の社会や世界を考えると、グローバル化の急速な進展がもたらす社会の変化によって、多くの若者が将来への不安を抱き、自信を失っているようにも見受けられます。大学は、そうした若者が希望を持って将来における自らの行動の指針を形成できる力を養う必要があります。そのために、大学は教養教育の在り方をもう一度振り返り、今こそその意義を取り戻すべきです。教養は人間にとっての糧、つまり生命力そのものだからです。

(通 訳)

10-7 | **Moderator 2**

Thank you for sharing these ideas with us. It seems that the liberal arts will continue to be very important in the future.

(通 訳)

⑩ Liberal Arts in a Globalized Age: What is the university's role?
大学の役割とは何か

academia	学界
consequences	結果
skepticism	懐疑心
defend	擁護する
complexity	複雑さ
recurring	繰り返し起きる
mimic (v.)	真似る
'deep learning'	「深層学習」
logical	論理的
trial and error	試行錯誤
multitude of perspectives	多角的な見方
solid liberal arts education	確立した教養教育
Albert Einstein (1879-1955)	アルベルト・アインシュタイン
practical education	実務教育
broad-based education	幅広い教育

危機に瀕す	under imminent threat
文部科学省	Ministry of Education, Culture, Sports, Science and Technology
大学設置基準	standards for establishing universities
緩和される	be relaxed
教養課程	general education courses
激減する	dramatically decrease
AI 化	turn to AI
切っても切れない関係	indispensable
養う	cultivate
言葉の起源	origin of the phrase
ギリシア・ローマ	Greece and Rome
理念的な源流	conceptual source
中世	Middle Ages
技芸	arts
根本的	fundamental
亀山郁夫学長（名古屋外国語大学）	President Kameyama (Nagoya University of Foreign Studies)
「エンパシー」	'empathy'
共感する能力	ability to empathize
急速な進展	rapid progress
不安を抱く	harbor insecurities
行動の指針	guiding principles for actions
振り返る	reflect
糧	nourishment
生命力	life

10-0　Moderator 1

次のトピックとして、技術が支配する世の中において、大学での教養教育の役割について、どのようにお考えですか。

10-1　English Speaker 1

学界は技術と人工知能の発展により、今世紀飛躍的な進歩を遂げました。この進歩は、学界のような社会的機関においても、様々な結果をもたらしています。多くの人が教養科目の目的について懐疑心を抱くようになり、大学は教養教育とその利点を擁護していかなければなりません。良識ある学生は、複雑ではあるが人間としての経験がいかに大切であるかを理解しています。そのような学生は、将来、物事を批判的に思考することのできる市民になるでしょう

10-2　English Speaker 2

人工知能を完成させるのに繰り返し起きる問題というのは、人工知能がまだ人間の知能を数学的方法を用いて真似ていることですが、それは「深層学習」と呼ばれ、論理に基づいています。しかし人間は常に論理的なわけではありません。むしろ、私たちは失敗や試行錯誤から問題を解決することができます。人工知能にはそれができません。このグローバル時代においては多角的な見方ができるので、せっかくの可能性を無視するのは賢明ではありません。確立した教養教育から得る幅広い知識の中にこそ、価値が隠れているのです。

10-3　Japanese Speaker 1

It could be said that liberal arts education in Japanese universities is currently under imminent threat. For one thing, at the beginning of the 1990s, according to Ministry of Education, Culture, Sports, Science and Technology policy, the standards for establishing universities were relaxed. As a result, universities' general education courses dramatically decreased. However, for those of us living in this age of globalization and the turn to AI, education is of course indispensable. The place to cultivate this education is naturally the university.

10-4　Japanese Speaker 2

The origin of the phrase 'liberal arts' has its conceptual source in Greece and Rome. In the European university system from the Middle Ages onward, it was regarded as the foundation of the arts that ought to be possessed by liberated humans. For current general education courses, the most fundamental and important thing is to cultivate the power of imagination towards others. Here at Nagoya University of Foreign Studies, President Kameyama uses the word 'empathy' to express this. In other words, education is to foster the ability to empathize with other people.

10-5　English Speaker 3

アルベルト・アインシュタインは、「教養教育のある大学の価値とは、ただ単に多くの事実を学ぶことではなく、考える力を養うことだ」と語りました。もし、実務教育の陰で教養教育が廃れていくと、学生たちは重要なものを得られなくなってしまいます。幅広い教育を受けると若者に選択肢の幅が広がり、それにより将来的に遭遇するであろう多くの複雑な難題にも対処できることになります。

10-6　Japanese Speaker 3

If we consider our future society and world, we may suppose that the majority of young people harbor insecurities about the future and may lose their confidence due to the changes in society brought about by the rapid progress of globalization. It is necessary for universities to take on such students' wishes and cultivate their power to form guiding principles for their actions. In order to do this, universities must reflect once again on what the liberal arts should be, and now especially must recover their significance. Education is nourishment for humanity; or, to put it another way, it is life itself.

10-7　Moderator 2

ご意見をお話しくださり、ありがとうございました。教養教育はこれから先も引き続き重要な役割を担っていきそうですね。

AI and humanity

人工知能と人間性

Keywords

Aldous Huxley (1894-1963)	心の余裕が生まれる
"Brave New World"	疲弊
satirical	強迫観念
dystopian	内在する
dehumanized	「つながりっぱなし」という弊害
socio-political	僻地
master-minded	素人
Soviet communism	画像を加工する
American capitalism	現代語
civilization	思惑を越える
benevolent	使いこなす
bureaucracy	価値観
discourage creativity	突き詰める
eugenics	便利さ
conformity	真のヒューマニティーを取り戻す
be content	課題
universal guaranteed income	
socially engaged	
revenue	

●-0 **English Speaker 1**

Aldous Huxley's book "Brave New World", written in 1932, is a satirical view of a dystopian world. It criticizes the course of human progress. In the book the future is a place where the individual has become dehumanized by a socio-political system. The system is master-minded by elites. The book was written at a time when Soviet communism and American capitalism were threatening to change civilization in ways unknown.

通 訳

-1　English Speaker 2

In the Brave New World, society functions with a <u>benevolent</u> <u>bureaucracy</u> that <u>discourages creativity</u>. Pleasures, feelings, and relationships are shallow. People are designed by <u>eugenics</u> to be satisfied with <u>conformity</u>. This makes for a public that is easy to control. People become <u>content</u> in lives of convenience where they are not encouraged to question anything too deeply.

(通　訳)

-2　Japanese Speaker 1

AI 技術がもたらす変化により、人間の生活は確かに便利になりました。しかし同時に、私たちは以前にもまして、ますます忙しくなったようにも思えます。本来であれば、技術の進化によって豊かな生活になったのだから、私たちにもっと<u>心</u>の余裕が<u>生まれる</u>はずです。それなのに、「新しい技術」が進化すればするほど、人が<u>疲弊</u>してしまうということは、常に AI 技術とつながっていなければならないという<u>強迫観念</u>が、現代の人々のどこかに<u>内在</u>しているからかもしれません。

(通　訳)

-3　Japanese Speaker 2

<u>「つながりっぱなし」</u>という<u>弊害</u>については、多くの人が実感している現実でしょう。今は、ネットにつながる環境さえあれば、どんな<u>僻地</u>にいても、昼夜かまわず仕事という日常が追いかけてくるようになりました。また、膨大な情報に溢れるネットを検索すれば、知らなくてもよいことまで、つい目に入ってきてしまうことも多々あります。さらに、写真や映像など、アプリケーションのおかげで、<u>素人</u>でもプロの写真家のように<u>画像</u>を<u>加工</u>できるようになり、いわゆる「インスタ映え」という<u>現代語</u>も日常で頻繁に耳にします。

(通　訳)

-4　English Speaker 3

In our Brave New World of the Internet there will be fewer jobs for people in in the future. What will people do for work? Finland is experimenting with a <u>universal guaranteed income</u> for those who cannot find work. But encouraging people to remain active and <u>socially engaged</u> is still the key to the program's success. Additionally, nations must ensure that the State or some other <u>revenue</u> source can provide support for such a society.

(通　訳)

Japanese Speaker 3

AI 自体は、今後も私たちの思惑を越えて発展し続けるのは確かです。ですが、その AI 技術をどのように使うか、そしてどう使いこなすかは、私たちの価値観がどちらに向かうかという選択によって決まってくると言えます。その選択を突き詰めるならば、「便利さ」と「幸福」のどちらを私たちの生活の中心に置くのか、ということになるでしょう。単にAI に依存するのではなく、来たるべき未来に向けて、私たちはどのような技術を選択し、またそれが人間に、また社会全体に真のヒューマニティーを取り戻すものであるかを考え続けることが、今後の私たちの課題となるでしょう。

通　訳

■ Simultaneous demonstration
AI and humanity
人工知能と人間性

Aldous Huxley (1894-1963)	オルダス・レナード・ハクスリー
"Brave New World"	『すばらしい新世界』
satirical	風刺的な
dystopian	ディストピアの（ユートピアに対して暗黒郷）
dehumanized	非人間的な
socio-political	社会政治的な
master-minded	操られる
Soviet communism	ソ連の共産主義
American capitalism	アメリカの資本主義
civilization	文明
benevolent	慈善的な
bureaucracy	官僚制度
discourage creativity	創造力を妨げる
eugenics	優生学
conformity	適合
be content	満足する
universal guaranteed income	最低所得保障制度
socially engaged	社会との繋がりを保つ
revenue	財源

心の余裕が生まれる	have room to breathe
疲弊	exhaustion
強迫観念	compulsive idea
内在する	be intrinsic
「つながりっぱなし」という弊害	harmful effects of 'constant connection'
僻地	backwater
素人	amateur (n.)
画像を加工する	create pictures
現代語	contemporary word
思惑を越える	exceed one's expectations
使いこなす	handle
価値観	value system
突き詰める	examine closely
便利さ	convenience
真のヒューマニティーを取り戻す	regain one's true humanity
課題	challenge (n.)

-0   English Speaker 1

オルダス・ハクスリーの本で、1932年に書かれた『すばらしい新世界』は、ディストピアの風刺的な考えです。それは人間の進歩の在り方を批判しています。その本の中では、未来とは個人が社会政治的な制度によって非人間的になる場所です。その制度は支配層によって陰で操られています。この本は、かつてソ連の共産主義とアメリカの資本主義が未知の方法で文明を変えようと脅かしていた時代に書かれました。

-1   English Speaker 2

「すばらしい新世界」のなかでは、社会は慈善的な官僚制度で機能しており、創造力を妨げています。喜び、感情、人間関係は希薄です。優生学のもとでは、人々は適合することに満足感を覚え、より支配されやすくなってしまいます。人々は物事を深く疑問に思うことなく、便利な生活に満足するようになります。

-2   Japanese Speaker 1

Humans' lives have certainly become convenient due to the changes brought about by AI technology. At the same time, we might also think we have become even busier than before. Strictly speaking, life has become richer through the progress of technology, so we ought to have more room to breathe. Nevertheless, the more 'new technology' advances, the more a compulsive idea that people's exhaustion must always be tied to AI technology seems to be intrinsic to humans today.

-3   Japanese Speaker 2

The reality is that many people really feel the harmful effects of 'constant connection'. These days, as long as you are connected to the Net, no matter what backwater you're in or what time of day or night, your daily routine of work will follow you. Further, if you search the net with its vast overflow of information, you may catch sight of many things you don't care to know. Moreover, thanks to apps for photos and videos, even amateurs can now create pictures like a professional, and we incessantly hear a contemporary word: the so-called *Instabae*.

-4   English Speaker 3

インターネット上における「すばらしい新世界」では、将来人々が担う仕事がどんどん減っていきます。人々は何を仕事にするのでしょうか。フィンランドでは、仕事につけない人々のために、最低所得保障制度の実験を行っています。しかし、人々が活発に行動し、社会との繋がりを保ち続けられるよう促進していけるかどうかが、この制度の成功の鍵となります。加えて、国家はそのような社会のために国やその他の財源を使って支援できるようにすべきです。

Japanese Speaker 3

It is certain that AI itself will continue to develop and <u>exceed our expectations</u> in future. However, it could be said that the questions of how AI technology will be used and how we will <u>handle</u> it will be decided by which way our <u>value system</u> leans. If we <u>examine</u> this choice <u>closely</u>, it will come down to whether we decide to emphasize '<u>convenience</u>' or 'happiness' in our lives. I believe our future <u>challenge</u> is not simply the existence of AI but what kind of future we should move towards, what kind of technology we should choose, and continued consideration of whether this will help us <u>regain our true humanity</u> — as people, and as society as a whole.

TOPIC 2:
An Era for Everyone

平成から令和への願い

❶ Terminology　用語の整理—元号とは

❷ The beginning of the Heisei period　平成の幕開け（1989年1月8日）

❸ Economy　バブルの崩壊（平成3年）

❹ Science　AI, IT の開発

❺ Religion　地下鉄サリン事件（平成9年）

❻ Politics　ポピュリズム政治（大衆迎合主義）と外交

❼ Natural Disasters　東日本大震災（2011年3月11日）

❽ Media　メディアの役割

❾ Literature　国境を超える文学とその役割

❿ Wishes for the Reiwa era　令和への願い（2019年5月1日）

■ Simultaneous demonstration
　Culture　平成が生んだポップカルチャー

第13回 学生通訳コンテスト スクリプト
2019年11月30日 開催

人だから成し得る通訳という作業

関沢　紘一
（学生通訳コンテスト審査員）

　名古屋外国語大学が行う「学生通訳コンテスト」は昨年11月に15回目を迎えました。2019年に我々の生活を一変させたコロナ禍の発生により、その開催と実施が危ぶまれましたが関係者の努力により工夫を重ね、中止されることなく毎年実施されてきました。人類の生命、人権、文化、科学技術等における情報交換の場である人間社会において不可欠な役割を果たす医療や司法における専門家通訳の育成の重要性は増すばかりです。司法通訳の話を例として挙げます。隣家との争いから、猟銃で一人を射殺し、他の一名に重傷を負わせるという殺人事件がありました。被疑者は英語を母国語とする男性でした。その被疑者の男性を日本の警察は連日取調べましたが、固く口を閉ざし、事件について語ろうとしませんでした。捜査当局は同事件の真相を知ることができず、捜査が行き詰ったとき、担当検察官がこの被疑者の取調べの通訳を代えて、再度取調べを開始しました。すると、通訳が交代したその日から、凄惨なその殺人事件について事件当時の自らの心理状態、動機、犯行状況の全てについての仔細を被疑者は包み隠さず自白し、遂に、事件の真相は解明をみたそうです。取調べに当たった検察官は、取調べの最後に、被疑者に「あなたは、ずっと警察の取り調べで黙秘していたのに、どうして、すべてを自白する気になったのですか」と尋ねたところ、被疑者は、「検察官の取調べの通訳に当たった通訳の方が私の話すことをきちんと聞いてくれ正確に通訳してくれて、この通訳を信頼できたので話す気になりました。」と検察官に答えたそうです。他方、世界的に著名なオーストラリアの医療通訳研究の権威は、「心臓外科の手術を行う医師の通訳人は、その外科医と同等の専門知識を持たなければ十全な医療通訳はできないだろう」と言っています。これらの話から、この社会が求める通訳の果たす役割の質と重要性が分かります。日常生活での簡単な通訳は、翻訳ソフトや、その他の携帯通訳器の便利さに頼ればある程度可能だとしても、大切な人命や人権が関わる状況や、国際間の重要な諸状況やビジネスにおいては、その専門性と真正な要求を満たせるのは、やはり生身の人間が表す感情、顔や目の動き、その発音や抑揚、強弱などからその言葉の真の意味を通訳できる「人」であると私は信じています。このワークブックは、「人」が行う通訳の実際が示されている貴重な資料といえるでしょう。

関沢　紘一 / Sekizawa, Koichi
西太平洋米海軍統合法務局（RLSO Westpac）国際法首席顧問（International Law Director）として、2022年3月、約半世紀の勤務ののち退職。在職中、日米間の司法当局の架け橋として多数の日米間の法律実務問題を扱い、日米両法廷の通訳も行う。その実績は両政府より高い評価を受けている。

1

Terminology

用語の整理—元号とは

Keywords

西暦	reign (n.)
「元号単位」	Gregorian Calendar
時代の象徴	Jesus Christ
中国の皇帝制度	Hijri Calendar
古典	monarch
『史記』	Victorian era (1837-1901)
『書経』	second Elizabethan era (1952-)
引用	Tudor (1485-1603)
天地	Windsor (1917-)
平和主義の志向	constitutional crisis
竹下登（1924-2000）	King Edward VIII (1894-1972)
日本最古の歌集『万葉集』	abdicate
出典	George VI (1936-1952)
「退位特例法」	
天皇の生前退位	
光格天皇（1771-1840）	
慶応（元号：1865-1868）	
縁起が悪い	
皇室典範	

1-0　Moderator 1

The beginning of a new era in Japan requires a lot of thought, as the name of the era contains hopes and wishes regarding what it will be like. How do other countries measure historical periods?

通　訳

1-1 Japanese Speaker 1

2019年4月30日、「平成」が終わり、翌日の5月1日から新しい時代である「令和」が始まりました。世界各国では西暦を用いますが、日本は時代としてとらえるときは「元号単位」で考えます。元号が変わると日本人の気持ちも空気も確実に変わると言われるほど、日本人にとって元号こそ時代の象徴を表すといっても過言ではありません。元号制度はもともとは中国の皇帝制度に由来するものです。ですから、元号は中国の古典からとって決めています。

通　訳

1-2 Japanese Speaker 2

ちなみに平成は、『史記』と『書経』から文言を引用したもので、「国の内外、また天地とも平和が達成される」という願いを込めて決められました。当時、平和主義の志向が強かった竹下登内閣らしい選択であったとも言われています。そして新元号「令和」は、日本最古の歌集、『万葉集』から引用され、初めて日本の古典が出典となりました。

通　訳

1-3 English Speaker 1

With each new reign, Japan returns to 'year 1'. At the same time, most Japanese people also use the western calendar. This is known as the 'Gregorian Calendar' and it is actually comparatively recent: it was only invented in the 16th century, and numbers the years according to the birth date of Jesus Christ. There are other ways of measuring years, too: Muslim countries use the 'Hijri Calendar' along with the Gregorian system to confirm the dates of religious events, while countries like Taiwan and North Korea have their own systems.

通　訳

1-4 English Speaker 2

Isn't it interesting how Japan connects its eras to literature! Another way of naming eras is to simply use the name of the ruling monarch. This is the system the U.K. uses: for example, the time in which Queen Victoria ruled is known as the Victorian era. Now the U.K. is in the second Elizabethan era. We can also name longer periods of history with the surname of the royal family: the 'Tudor' period covers five different kings and queens, all with the surname 'Tudor'. Now we are in the 'Windsor' period. Of course, this means we cannot give the name of the era a deep meaning in the same way Japan does.

(通 訳)

1-5 Japanese Speaker 3

2017年6月、日本で「退位特例法」が成立し、平成が終わることが決まりました。これは天皇の生前退位を認める特例法です。歴史を遡ると、生前退位は江戸時代の光格天皇以来、200年ぶりのことです。実は明治の前の慶応までは、何度でも元号を変えることができました。大きな災害などがあったりすると「縁起が悪い」といって、元号が変更されてきました。皇室典範は伝統に従いながらも、今後、時代に合わせて変わっていくのかもしれません。

(通 訳)

1-6 English Speaker 3

In the U.K. we had our own constitutional crisis: in 1936 King Edward VIII wanted to marry an American woman with whom he had fallen in love. However, she had been divorced twice and under Church of England rules the King was not allowed to marry her. Although Edward faced great pressure to give up, he would not. He abdicated and got married instead, and his younger brother George became King. George VI was the father of our current Queen, who has now reigned longer than any other British monarch.

(通 訳)

1-7 Moderator 2

Our calendars and ways of measuring history can tell us a lot about our cultures. Further, changes to rules like abdication can show us new trends and possibilities in wider society.

(通 訳)

❶ Terminology
用語の整理―元号とは

西暦	Western calendar
「元号単位」	'era names as a unit'
時代の象徴	representative symbol of the era
中国の皇帝制度	China's imperial system
古典	classics
『史記』	"The Historical Records"
『書経』	"The Book of Documents"
引用	quotation
天地	heaven and earth
平和主義の志向	towards pacifism
竹下登（1924-2000）	the Noboru Takeshita cabinet
日本最古の歌集『万葉集』	the oldest Japanese collection of songs ("Man'yōshū")
出典	source (n.)
「退位特例法」	'Special Exception Concerning Abdication law'
天皇の生前退位	abdication of the emperor
光格天皇（1771-1840）	Emperor Kōkaku
慶応（元号：1865-1868）	the Keiō era
縁起が悪い	bad omen
皇室典範	the Imperial House Act

reign (n.)	在位
Gregorian Calendar	グレゴリオ暦
Jesus Christ	イエス・キリスト
Hijri Calendar	イスラム暦
monarch	君主
Victorian era (1837-1901)	ヴィクトリア時代
second Elizabethan era (1952-)	エリザベス女王二世の時代
Tudor (1485-1603)	チューダー朝
Windsor (1917-)	ウィンザー朝
constitutional crisis	憲政の危機
King Edward VIII (1894-1972)	エドワード8世
abdicate	王位を譲る
George VI (1936-1952)	ジョージ6世

Moderator 1

日本での新しい時代の幕開けというものは、年号にその時代がどのようになるのかという期待や願いが込められています。他の国々ではどのように時代を分けているのでしょうか。

Japanese Speaker 1

On April 30, 2019, the era 'Heisei' came to an end and a new era, 'Reiwa', began the next day, May 1. Many countries around the world utilise the <u>Western calendar</u>. Japan, however, thinks of historical eras using '<u>era names as a unit</u>'. When a new era arrives, it is not an exaggeration to claim that the change brings Japanese people a new kind of mentality and atmosphere, which means the era name is the <u>representative symbol of that era</u>. The naming system of eras stems from <u>China's imperial system</u>. Therefore, the names have been chosen from Chinese <u>classics</u>.

Japanese Speaker 2

Further, the Heisei era was decided by a <u>quotation</u> from "<u>The Historical Records</u>" and "<u>The Book of Documents</u>", containing wishes for "the achievement of inner and outer peace on <u>heaven and earth</u>". It is said that this was a characteristic choice of <u>the Noboru Takeshita cabinet</u>, whose leaned <u>towards pacifism</u> at the time. Then, the name of the new era 'Reiwa' was referenced from <u>the Japanese oldest collection of songs, the "Man'yōshū"</u>. It was the first time a Japanese classic was used as the <u>source</u>.

English Speaker 1

新たな天皇の<u>在位</u>により、暦は元年へと戻ります。和暦と共に、日本人は西暦も使用します。これは<u>グレゴリオ暦</u>として知られており、比較的近年の16世紀から使用され、<u>イエス・キリスト</u>の誕生から年数が数えられています。暦の測り方には他の方法もあります。イスラム世界では<u>イスラム暦</u>が、宗教的祭事を確認するために、グレゴリオ暦と共に用いられます。また、台湾や北朝鮮といった国々には、独自の年号制度があります。

English Speaker 2

日本における元号と文学の関わり合いは興味深いですね。単にその時代を統治している<u>君主</u>の名前を元号につけるという決め方もあります。イギリスでは、この方法で元号を決めています。例えば、ヴィクトリア女王が統治した時代は<u>ヴィクトリア時代</u>として知られています。現在のイギリスは<u>エリザベス女王二世</u>の時代です。私たちイギリス人は歴史上、より長期にわたる時代は王族の苗字を名付けることがあるのです。<u>チューダー朝</u>においては、5人の王と女王全員がチューダーの苗字を持つことになります。現在私たちは<u>ウィンザー朝</u>の時代を生きており、もちろん、これは日本のように年号に深い意味を与えるわけではないことを意味しています。

1-5   Japanese Speaker 3

In June 2017, the 'Special Exception Concerning Abdication law' was established in Japan and it was determined that the Heisei era would end. This was a special exception law recognising the abdication of the emperor. If we look back through history, it has been 200 years since the last abdication of an emperor, Emperor Kōkaku in the Edo era. As a matter of fact, before the Meiji era, up until the Keiō era, the name of the era could be changed any number of times. The name would be changed if 'bad omens' such as large disasters occurred. The Imperial House Act follows tradition; however, it may change with the times from now on.

1-6   English Speaker 3

イギリスでも憲政の危機がありました。1936年、エドワード8世がアメリカ人女性と恋に落ち、結婚を望みました。しかし、その女性は2度の離婚経験があったため、イギリス国教会の規則により、彼女との結婚は許されませんでした。エドワード王は、結婚を諦めるという強い反対にも関わらず、結婚を諦めなかったのです。結婚を選び、弟のジョージに王位を譲りました。ジョージ6世は現在の女王の父にあたります。エリザベス女王は、歴代最長のイギリス君主です。

1-7   Moderator 2

和暦と歴史の区切りは、私たちの文化と深く結びついているのです。さらには、退位などの規則の変更は、社会の新しい流れや可能性を示しています。

2

The beginning of the Heisei period

平成の幕開け（1989年1月8日）

Keywords

Communist	天安門事件（1989年6月4日）
Czechoslovakia	天安門広場
Romania	民主化を求める
Soviet Union (1922-1991)	中国人民解放軍
President Frederik Willem de Klerk (1936-)	武力で弾圧する
	ノーベル平和賞
regime	劉暁波（りゅうぎょうは：1955-2017）
racist	撤退する
Apartheid (1948-1991)	消費税
be impacted	税率
exaggeration	リクルート事件（1988年）
isolation	官僚
transformative	政官界
	未公開株
	有力者
	政治改革
	転換期を迎える
	ベルリンの壁が崩壊する
	東西冷戦
	終結に向かう
	明るい兆しを見せる
	バブル経済が崩壊し始める
	右上がり
	景気の失速
	突入する

2-0   **Moderator 1**

The Heisei era was named with the hope of achieving 'peace everywhere'. But can this be achieved so easily?

通 訳

2-1   **English Speaker 1**

If we look at the first year of the Heisei era in a global context, we can see that there was a worldwide move towards democracy. In Europe the Berlin Wall, which had divided democratic West and Communist East Germany for years, was opened in 1989, the first year of the Heisei era; revolutions in Czechoslovakia and Romania installed democratic governments; finally, in 1991, the Soviet Union was ended.

通 訳

2-2   **English Speaker 2**

There was also progress in other parts of the world. In 1989 Brazil had its first democratic election for a president in 29 years. South Africa also had a new president, de Klerk, in 1989, whose regime began to take apart the racist 'Apartheid' system that had separated white and non-white people in the country since 1948. In all these changes we can see a trend in the direction of democracy and an ideal of rights for all people.

通 訳

2-3   **Japanese Speaker 1**

その一方で、中国では1989年6月4日に天安門事件が起こりました。これは、北京の天安門広場に民主化を求める学生たちが集結したことに対し、中国人民解放軍が武力で弾圧した事件です。2017年、ノーベル平和賞を受賞した劉暁波（りゅうぎょうは）氏が亡くなりましたが、彼は学生たちが安全に撤退できるように軍と交渉し暴力の拡大を防いだ人物でした。

通 訳

2-4 Japanese Speaker 2

日本では平成元年、消費税が導入されます。当時の税率は3%でした。消費税はリクルート事件という政治家や官僚を巻き込んだ大スキャンダルが拡大する中で導入されました。リクルート社の社長が政官界へ影響を与えることを狙い、未公開株を政治家などの有力者にばらまいたのがリクルート事件です。多くの政治家は実際にその株を売却して多額の利益を得ました。この事件により、政治改革が叫ばれるようになります。

通 訳

2-5 English Speaker 3

As the last example shows, it's important to recognize that major events in political, financial, or social fields can affect the everyday lives of citizens as well as the leaders of society. Students, teachers, and ordinary consumers have all been impacted by these events. And it's no exaggeration to say that none of these huge changes happens in isolation: for example, financial changes influence politics, political events shape the law, etc. We need to recognize the complex system that determines whether or not we can live in peace.

通 訳

2-6 Japanese Speaker 3

平成という時代の幕開けは、さまざまな意味で歴史が大きな転換期を迎えた時でした。海外ではベルリンの壁が崩壊し、東西冷戦が終結に向かい、国際情勢が明るい兆しを見せていました。その一方で、国内ではバブル経済が崩壊し始め、戦後、右上がりにしか経験したことのなかった日本の経済が、その後長く続く景気の失速へと突入していく時代でもあったのです。

通 訳

2-7 Moderator 2

The beginning of the Heisei era saw major changes leading to reforms in Japanese society; beyond Japan, it was a transformative few years for the entire world.

通 訳

② The beginning of the Heisei period
平成の幕開け（1989年1月8日）

Communist	共産主義の
Czechoslovakia	チェコスロバキア
Romania	ルーマニア
Soviet Union (1922-1991)	ソビエト連邦（ソ連）
President Frederik Willem de Klerk (1936-)	ウィリアム・デ・クラーク大統領
regime	政権
racist	人種差別的な
Apartheid (1948-1991)	アパルトヘイト
be impacted	影響を受ける
exaggeration	過言
isolation	単独
transformative	転換期の

天安門事件（1989年6月4日）	the Tiananmen Incident
天安門広場	Tiananmen Square
民主化を求める	seek democratisation
中国人民解放軍	People's Liberation Army
武力で弾圧する	use military force to oppress
ノーベル平和賞	the Nobel Peace Prize
劉暁波（りゅうぎょうは：1955-2017）	Liu Xiaobo
撤退する	withdraw
消費税	consumption tax
税率	tax rate
リクルート事件（1988年）	the Recruit Incident
官僚	bureaucrat
政官界	political world
未公開株	unlisted shares
有力者	influential person
政治改革	political reform
転換期を迎える	encounter transition
ベルリンの壁が崩壊する	Berlin wall is demolished
東西冷戦	Cold War
終結に向かう	draw to an end
明るい兆しを見せる	show encouraging bright signs
バブル経済が崩壊し始める	Bubble economy begins to collapse
右上がり	growth
景気の失速	downturn
突入する	plunge into

2-0　Moderator 1

平成という元号は、いかなる場所でも平和を実現するという願いを込めて名づけられました。しかし、その願いはそれほど簡単に叶えられるものなのでしょうか。

2-1　English Speaker 1

世界的な視野で平成元年を振り返ると、民主化に向けた世界的な動きがみられます。ヨーロッパでは、民主主義の西ドイツと共産主義の東ドイツを何年にもわたり隔ててきたベルリンの壁が、平成元年の1989年に崩壊しました。さらにチェコスロバキアでは革命が起き、ルーマニアでは民主的な政府が設立されました。そしてついにソビエト連邦が1991年に終焉を迎えました。

2-2　English Speaker 2

また、世界の他の地域でも民主化への動きが見られました。1989年にブラジルでは、実に29年ぶりとなる民主的な大統領選が行われました。南アフリカでは1989年に新たにウィリアム・デ・クラーク大統領が誕生しました。1948年から続いた白色人種と有色人種を隔離する人種差別的なアパルトヘイトの廃止に向けた動きがその政権下で始まりました。こうした変化から、さらなる民主化への流れと、すべての人々が持つべき理想的な権利のあり方が見えてきたのです。

2-3　Japanese Speaker 1

On the other hand, on June 4, 1989, in China, the Tiananmen Incident occurred. This is the incident which the Chinese army – the so-called People's Liberation Army – used military force to oppress Chinese students gathered at Tiananmen Square to seek the democratisation of their government. In 2017, Liu Xiaobo, who was awarded the Nobel Peace Prize, passed away. He was a person who negotiated with the Chinese army and prevented the expansion of violence so that the students could safely withdraw from the scene.

2-4　Japanese Speaker 2

In the first year of Heisei, consumption tax was introduced in Japan. The tax rate was 3% at the time. The tax system was introduced while a large scandal, the Recruit Incident, which involved politicians and bureaucrats, was expanding. That incident was caused by the president of a company, Recruit, who aimed to have an effect on the political world by widely distributing the company's unlisted shares to influential persons. In reality, many politicians gained a great deal of profit by selling those shares. The incident triggered strong demands for political reform from the public.

2-5 English Speaker 3

最後の例が示すように、政治、金融、社会分野の主な出来事はすべての人々の生活、または社会の指導者たちへも影響を与えうるということを認識することが、大切なことなのです。学生、教師、そして一般の消費者すべてがこれらの出来事から影響を受けています。そして、このような社会的変化は決して単独で起こるものではないといっても過言ではありません。例えば、金融の変化は政治に影響を与え、政治的な出来事により法律にも変化をもたらします。私たちは、平和に生活を送れるかどうかを決定づけるこういった複雑なシステムを理解しておく必要があるのです。

2-6 Japanese Speaker 3

The beginning of the Heisei era was a moment when history encountered massive transition in various contexts. Overseas the Berlin wall was demolished, the Cold War was drawing to its end, and international affairs had showed some encouraging bright signs. Meanwhile, in Japan the Bubble economy began to collapse, and it was also a time when the Japanese economy – which had experienced only growth since the end of WW2 – was plunging into a downturn.

2-7 Moderator 2

平成の幕開けでは日本社会、そして諸外国において改革を引き起こすような大きな変化がみられる時代であり、世界全体にとっての転換期であったのです。

3
Economy
バブルの崩壊（平成3年）

Keywords

バブル景気に沸く	upheaval
貿易摩擦	stagnation
円安	'Lost Decade'
輸出産業	dominant
貿易黒字国	financial crisis
自国製品	stock market
低迷する	Wall Street Crash (1929)
景気悪化	the Great Depression (1929-1939)
深刻化する	Lehman Shock (2008)
「プラザ合意」（1985年、ニューヨーク）	endure
G5諸国（米、英、仏、西独、日）	'job for life'
締結する	sense of identity
円高不況に陥る	in favour of
金融政策	benefit (n.)
地価	make redundant
株価	
高騰する	
日本銀行	
急激な下落	
煽りを受ける	
派遣社員	
非正規労働者	
正社員	
解雇する	
通告する	
打ち切る	
「派遣切り」	
労働者の雇用問題	

3-0　Moderator 1

The beginning of the Heisei era saw huge changes in Japan's economy. As the years went on, major global <u>upheavals</u> threatened the financial stability of the developed world.

通　訳

3-1　Japanese Speaker 1

1989年の平成元年、日本は<u>バブル景気に</u>沸いていました。その始まりは、アメリカと日本との間に生じた<u>貿易摩擦</u>です。1980年代の前半、日本は<u>円安</u>の影響を受けて<u>輸出産業</u>が伸び、<u>貿易黒字国</u>となっていました。一方アメリカは、<u>自国製品</u>の売り上げが<u>低迷</u>し、<u>景気悪化</u>が<u>深刻化</u>していました。

通　訳

3-2　Japanese Speaker 2

その後、アメリカの景気改善を目指し、1985年にニューヨークで「<u>プラザ合意</u>」が<u>G5</u>諸国の間で<u>締結</u>されます。結果、今度は日本が<u>円高不況</u>に陥り、その不況改善のために大幅な<u>金融政策</u>を行ったことでバブル経済が生まれたのです。日本国内では<u>地価</u>や<u>株価</u>は高騰し続け、政府や<u>日本銀行</u>は1990年に改めて金融政策を行いましたが、逆に地価や株価の急激な<u>下落</u>を招き、1991年にバブルが崩壊しました。

通　訳

3-3　English Speaker 1

Following the collapse of Japan's Bubble Economy came ten years of economic <u>stagnation</u> known as '<u>the Lost Decade</u>'. Japan's GDP fell, while workers' wages stopped rising, and many regular employees were replaced by temporary workers. The country has never reached the same level of spending as during the Bubble period. In terms of industry, <u>dominant</u> Japanese brands like Toyota and Sony began to face big competition from other East Asian brands. We can say that the Bubble bursting dramatically changed the lives of ordinary Japanese people.

通　訳

3-4 English Speaker 2

But this collapse was not the first time a <u>financial crisis</u> has changed an entire country, or even the world. The collapse of the U.S. <u>stock market</u> in October 1929 is known as the 'Wall Street Crash', and it led to huge economic problems throughout the western world. In America unemployment rose to 24%; it became known as <u>the Great Depression</u>. More recently, in 2008, another global crisis hit, and the world financial system was close to collapse. This <u>Lehman Shock</u> affected both the western and Asian economies.

通 訳

3-5 Japanese Speaker 3

当然、日本も2008年のリーマンショックから深刻な影響を受けました。自動車の生産が激減し、その煽りを受けたのが派遣社員などの非正規労働者です。正社員を解雇するときは30日前に通告する義務がありますが、派遣社員に対してはその必要はありません。そのため、突然、契約の更新をしないというかたちで契約を打ち切られる「派遣切り」に遭う人が続出しました。それから10年以上経た現在もその影響がすべての労働者の雇用問題のなかに残っています。

通 訳

3-6 English Speaker 3

That's right. The financial crises that Japan has <u>endured</u> have caused major changes in employment. The idea of a 'job for life', which provided security and a strong <u>sense of identity</u>, is disappearing <u>in favour of</u> temporary workers. While there are advantages to introducing more flexible working styles and increasing the number of working women, temporary workers often do not have <u>benefits</u> like holiday time and pensions, and they can be <u>made redundant</u> at any time. These issues are also affecting the U.K. and many other countries.

通 訳

3-7 Moderator 2

If there is one thing to remember about the impact of financial crises like the Bubble bursting and the Lehman Shock, it's that they affect the everyday lives of ordinary people most of all.

通 訳

③ Economy
バブルの崩壊（平成3年）

バブル景気に沸く	Bubble economy gets into hot water
貿易摩擦	trade friction
円安	depreciation of the yen
輸出産業	export industry
貿易黒字国	trade surplus country
自国製品	domestic product
低迷する	sluggish
景気悪化	economic downturn
深刻化する	become serious
「プラザ合意」（1985年、ニューヨーク）	Plaza Agreement
G5諸国（米、英、仏、西独、日）	G5 nations
締結する	conclude
円高不況に陥る	fall into a recession with the appreciation of the yen
金融政策	monetary policy
地価	land price
株価	stock price
高騰する	rise steeply
日本銀行	Bank of Japan
急激な下落	quick drop
煽りを受ける	negative effects impact
派遣社員	people in non-regular employment
非正規労働者	temporary worker
正社員	regular worker
解雇する	dismiss
通告する	inform
打ち切る	cancel
「派遣切り」	downsizing by laying off part-time or temporary workers (*hakengiri*)
労働者の雇用問題	employment problems for workers
upheaval	激変
stagnation	低迷
'Lost Decade'	「失われた10年」
dominant	代表的な
financial crisis	金融危機
stock market	株式市場
Wall Street Crash (1929)	ウォール街の崩壊
the Great Depression (1929-1939)	世界恐慌
Lehman Shock (2008)	リーマンショック
endure	見舞われる
'job for life'	「終身雇用」
sense of identity	帰属精神
in favour of	～を優先する
benefit (n.)	恩恵
make redundant	解雇する

3-0　Moderator 1

平成の幕開けには日本経済での大きな変化がみられました。時が経つにつれ、世界的な激変で先進国の金融の安定性が脅かされました。

3-1　Japanese Speaker 1

In 1989, the first year of Heisei, Japan's Bubble economy was getting into hot water. The beginning was trade friction between Japan and the United States. In the first half of the 1980s Japan became a trade surplus country whose export industry grew with the influence of the depreciation of the yen. On the other hand, in the United States, the sale of their domestic products was sluggish and their economic downturn was becoming serious.

3-2　Japanese Speaker 2

After that, in order to improve the economic situation of the U.S.A., the Plaza Agreement was concluded in NY in 1985 among the G5 nations. As the result of the agreement, Japan fell into a recession with the appreciation of the yen. In order to combat this depression major monetary policies were enacted, and thus the Bubble Economy was born. Domestic land and stock prices continued to rise steeply: in 1990 the government and Bank of Japan enacted another monetary policy, but this led conversely to quick drops in the value of land and stocks. In 1991, the Bubble collapsed.

3-3　English Speaker 1

バブル経済の崩壊に続く10年間の景気の低迷は「失われた10年」として知られています。労働者の賃金が上がらなくなったのと同時に、日本のGDPは下落し、多くの正社員が派遣社員にとって代わりました。日本はバブルの時のような消費レベルに戻ることはありませんでした。産業に関しては、日本の代表企業であるトヨタやソニーが東アジアの大企業との競争に直面し始めたのです。バブルの崩壊により、日本人の暮らしは劇的に変化しました。

3-4　English Speaker 2

しかし、バブル崩壊で国全体もしくは世界が金融危機に陥ったのは、この時が初めてではありません。1929年10月に起こったアメリカの株式市場崩壊は「ウォール街の崩壊」として知られています。その金融危機は、欧米諸国全体に大きな経済問題を引き起こしました。アメリカ国内の失業率は24％まで上昇し、それが世界恐慌として知られるようになりました。近年では、2008年に再び世界的危機が襲い、世界の金融システムは危うく崩壊しかけました。このリーマンショックは欧米諸国とアジア諸国の経済に影響を与えました。

3-5   Japanese Speaker 3

As a matter of fact, Japan was also seriously affected by the Lehman Brothers bankruptcy in 2008. The production of domestic cars declined terribly. The <u>negative effects impacted people in non-regular employment</u>, including <u>temporary workers</u>. In order to <u>dismiss</u> <u>regular workers</u>, companies are supposed to <u>inform</u> them of their layoffs up to 30 days beforehand. They do not have such a duty towards dispatched workers from agency companies. Therefore, many workers encountered *hakengiri,* <u>(downsizing by laying off part-time or temporary workers)</u>, being suddenly told that their contracts would be not renewed or would be <u>cancelled</u>. Even though it has been ten years since that time, the effect of this social phenomenon still remains in <u>employment problems for all workers</u>.

3-6   English Speaker 3

そのとおりです。日本は金融危機に見舞われましたが、それが原因で雇用形態が大きく変化しました。安心感や会社に所属するという帰属精神を与えていた「終身雇用」という考えが、派遣社員を優先することによって失われつつあります。より柔軟な働き方を導入することや、働く女性を増やすことの利点がある一方、派遣社員は休暇や年金という恩恵を受けられなかったり、いつでも解雇されうるのです。これらの問題はイギリスや他の数多くの国々にも影響を与えています。

3-7   Moderator 2

バブルの崩壊やリーマンショックのような金融危機の影響について心に留めておくことがあるとすれば、金融危機は多くの一般人の生活に影響を与えるということなのです。

4

Science

AI, IT の開発

4-0　Moderator 1

In terms of science the Heisei era brought the greatest changes to our lives since the Industrial Revolution. This was thanks to the spread of the computer and the Internet.

通　訳

4 -1 English Speaker 1

Through the progress of IT, advances in AI have raised important philosophical questions about consciousness and humanity, and how we deal with AI in areas like war and labour must be thought about very carefully. AI is also becoming part of our everyday lives and hobbies, and it seems we will not be able to avoid it in future even if we want to, so we should try to recognize its positive points. For example, lately many articles have been published about the use of AI in the 2020 Tokyo Olympics.

通 訳

4 -2 English Speaker 2

The Olympics will use various 'robot assistants' designed by Toyota: robots for collecting sports equipment thrown by competitors, and a moving robot carrying a human-size screen so that people can attend the event virtually. Judges in the gymnastics competitions will be helped by AI assistants that can assess the skill of the athletes. AI surveillance systems may also be used to provide security: they can identify people acting suspiciously, as well as people with disabilities who might need extra help travelling around Tokyo.

通 訳

4 -3 Japanese Speaker 1

平成は、情報技術が一段と進化し、インターネットや人工知能が社会に様々な影響を与えた時代でした。1995年11月23日の午前0時、アメリカのマイクロソフト社が発売した「Windows 95」の日本語版の販売が始まり、この年は「インターネット元年」と呼ばれました。深夜だというのに、秋葉原はいち早く「Windows 95」を購入したい人々が入り乱れ、大騒ぎになったことは未だ記憶に新しく残っています。

通 訳

4 -4 **Japanese Speaker 2**

今では個人の<u>ネット利用率</u>は8割を超えますが、1995年はまだパソコンは一般家庭にはほとんど普及していませんでした。<u>ビジネスシーン</u>でも当時はインターネットが全く使われておらず、携帯電話が一般に普及し始めたのもちょうどこの時期のことです。1990年代初期、携帯電話を利用するには、<u>加入料</u>の4万5,800円に加えて<u>保証金</u>10万円が必要という、今では考えられない<u>使用条件</u>が課されていました。

(通 訳)

4 -5 **English Speaker 3**

We can see that developments in IT and AI have changed the way we communicate, who we can communicate with, and what communication means. In terms of spreading knowledge of Japan to the world IT has been key, allowing people to share Japanese culture and make Japanese friends even if they haven't visited the country. Further, the use of AI in events like the Tokyo Olympics, as well as the Japanese companies at the <u>cutting edge</u> of AI, are helping strengthen Japan's reputation as a highly technological nation.

(通 訳)

4 -6 **Japanese Speaker 3**

IT、AIの普及が私たちの生活をより便利なものにしてくれる一方で、2017年に<u>内閣府</u>が発表した<u>世論調査</u>の結果は、現代人である私たちに問いを投げかけるものでした。それは、<u>犯罪に遭う</u>かもしれない場所を人々に尋ねたところ、「インターネット空間」と答えた人が6割以上に上ったということです。誰もが<u>不特定多数</u>を相手に「<u>表現者</u>」になりえる<u>ネット時代</u>において、<u>悪意を持て</u>ば、ネットが危険な道具と化す恐れがあることを、私たちは忘れてはいけません。

(通 訳)

4 -7 **Moderator 2**

The introduction of IT and AI in the Heisei era has changed our lives forever, and we should think carefully about their positive and negative effects.

(通 訳)

④ Science
AI, IT の開発

philosophical	哲学的な
consciousness	意識
humanity	人間らしさ
competitor	相手選手
virtually	視覚的に
gymnastics	体操競技
surveillance system	監視システム
suspiciously	不審に
people with disabilities	障害者
cutting edge	最先端

一段と進化する	advance further
人工知能	AI (artificial intelligence)
「インターネット元年」	'first year of the Internet'
入り乱れる	bustle (v.)
ネット利用率	Internet usage rate
ビジネスシーン	business setting
加入料	subscription fee
保証金	deposit
条件を課す	impose conditions
内閣府	Cabinet
世論調査	public opinion poll
犯罪に遭う	be associated with crime
不特定多数	many unidentified people
表現者	artist
ネット時代	Internet age
悪意を持つ	have bad intentions

4-0　Moderator 1

科学に関しては、産業革命以来、平成という時代は私たちの生活に多大な変化をもたらしました。これはコンピューターとインターネットの普及によるものです。

4-1　English Speaker 1

情報技術の進歩を通して、人工知能の進化は人間の意識や人間らしさという重要な哲学的な問題を提起してきました。そして、私たちがどのように人工知能を戦争や労働などの分野で扱うのかは、注意深く考慮しなければなりません。人工知能は私たちの毎日の生活と趣味の一部となってきており、将来、私たちにとって避けたくても避けられないものとなることでしょう。ですから、私たちは人工知能の利点を知ろうとしなければならないのです。例えば、最近では2020年の東京オリンピックでの人工知能の使い方について書かれた多くの記事が出ています。

4-2　English Speaker 2

オリンピックでは、トヨタ社によって設計された様々な「補助ロボット」が使用されます。相手選手が投げたスポーツ用具を拾うロボットや、観客が視覚的に競技を観戦できるように人間サイズのスクリーンを運ぶロボットもあります。体操競技の審査には、人工知能がアスリートの技術を評価する補助係として活躍することでしょう。人工知能による監視システムは、安全面でも利用できます。不審な行動をしている人々を特定したり、東京辺りを移動するのに手助けを必要としている障害者も見つけたりすることができるのです。

4-3　Japanese Speaker 1

Heisei was an era in which IT advanced further, and the Internet and AI had various effects on society. At midnight on November 23, 1995, an American firm, Microsoft, began selling the Japanese version of Windows 95. This year was called the 'first year of the Internet'. Even though it was late at night, people looking forward to purchasing Windows 95 gathered in Akihabara. The bustle in the city still remains as a fresh memory in people's minds.

4-4　Japanese Speaker 2

These days the personal Internet usage rate is over 80%, but in 1995 PCs were not really spread in ordinary households. In business settings the Internet wasn't used at all, and it was the time when mobile phone use had just started among ordinary people. At the beginning of the 1990's, in order to utilise mobile phones people had incredible conditions imposed on them: 45,800 yen subscription fees and 100,000 yen as a deposit.

4-5　English Speaker 3

情報技術、人工知能の分野での発展が、私たちのコミュニケーション方法、誰とコミュニケーションをするのかということ、コミュニケーションが意味するものを変化させてきたのがわかります。日本の知識を世界に発信する点に関して、IT は重要な役割を果たしてきました。IT のおかげで、日本を訪問したことのない人でも日本の文化を知り、日本の友達を作ることができるようになりました。さらに、東京オリンピックのような機会に AI を使用することにより、日本企業の最先端の AI 技術を示すことになり、日本が高度な技術大国であるという評判も高めることになるでしょう。

4-6　Japanese Speaker 3

While the spread of IT and AI have made our lives more convenient, the results of a public opinion poll announced by the Cabinet in 2017 raised questions among people like us living in this modern age. This was the fact that, when asked about places that could be associated with crime, 60% of the respondents answered 'the Internet'. In an Internet age in which any person can be an 'artist' performing for many unidentified people, if they have bad intentions the Internet can turn out to be a dangerous tool. We must not forget this.

4-7　Moderator 2

平成の IT と AI の導入は私たちの生活に半永久的な変化をもたらしましたが、IT と AI の良い点や悪い点についても注意深く考えていかなければいけません。

5

Religion

地下鉄サリン事件（平成9年）

Keywords

オウム真理教	secularization
「松本サリン事件」（1994年6月27日）	fundamentalism
新興宗教団体	cult activity
ヨガ道場	religious extremism
住民が訴訟を起こす	9/11 attacks of 2001
松本地方裁判所	Islamic extremist group Al-Qaeda
裁判官官舎	Muslims
サリンを撒く	offshoot
犠牲となる	'new religions'
「地下鉄サリン事件」（1995年3月20日）	genuine
出勤時間	charismatic
吸引する	brainwashing
駅員	Scientology
教祖	pros and cons
高学歴	ex-members
入信する	crucial
大規模に及ぶ	
そこはかとない不安	
充満する	
「生きづらさ」	
負の遺産	

5 -0　　Moderator 1

The Heisei era was a very interesting time for religion: it saw rises in secularization, religious fundamentalism, and cult activity. Let's look at some examples.

通　訳

5-1 | Japanese Speaker 1

1994年6月、オウム真理教により「松本サリン事件」が起きました。オウム真理教は新興宗教団体で、1990年代に全国各地にヨガ道場を展開していたため、長野県松本市に施設を作ろうとしたところ、住民訴訟が起こります。それに対して、教団は松本地方裁判所の裁判官官舎に向けてサリンを撒き、その結果、学生や会社員など8名が犠牲となりました。

通 訳

5-2 | Japanese Speaker 2

翌年の1995年3月20日に、オウムは「地下鉄サリン事件」を起こします。ちょうど出勤時間を狙い、都心の地下鉄車内でサリンが撒かれました。それを吸引した被害者は次々と倒れ、乗客、そして駅員ら13人が命を落とし、約6,000名が被害に遭い、当時の日本社会に大きな衝撃を与えました。その後、教祖の麻原彰晃は逮捕され、教団には多くの若者、特に高学歴を持つ若者が入信していたことがわかりました。

通 訳

5-3 | English Speaker 1

That must have been a terrible event for Japan! It's also very interesting, because it includes two major trends that have been connected with religion in the Heisei era: terrorism connected to religious extremism, and cult activity. I think everyone knows about the 9/11 attacks of 2001 in New York, when the Islamic extremist group Al-Qaeda destroyed the World Trade Center. Almost 3,000 people were killed and 6,000 injured. Unfortunately, this event created an unfair and negative image of ordinary Muslims that continues to this day.

通 訳

5-4 **English Speaker 2**

As well as extremist offshoots of major religions, the Heisei era saw an increase in so-called 'new religions', many of which are thought of as cults. How do we tell the difference between a genuine religion and a cult? First, cults often require you to pay money to join or make progress. Second, they generally have a charismatic leader. Third, they do not allow you to leave easily, and use brainwashing techniques to stop you thinking clearly. Aum Shinrikyo was the major cult in Japan during this period; in the West it was Scientology, which has famous people like the actor Tom Cruise as members.

通 訳

5-5 **Japanese Speaker 3**

オウム真理教がこのような大規模に及ぶ恐ろしい事件を起こしたその目的とは一体何だったのでしょうか。当時、バブル崩壊後の日本社会には、そこはかとない不安が世の中に充満していました。そんな時に、人を引き付ける何かを持っていたのがオウム真理教だったのかもしれません。多くの若者がこの教団に入信したのも、その背景には、バブル景気とその崩壊の裏で確実に募っていた「生きづらさ」という日本社会がもたらした負の遺産があったのです。

通 訳

5-6 **English Speaker 3**

The spread of the Internet and social media in the second part of the Heisei era has both pros and cons for extremism and cult activity. For example, in the late 1990s Scientology became less popular, because ex-members could easily share their negative experiences online and people could learn about its dangers. On the other hand, social media also makes it easier for cults and terrorist groups to advertise to and contact new members. This is why it's crucial for young people especially to think critically about information they see online!

通 訳

5-7 **Moderator 2**

Religion is a difficult subject to discuss in many parts of the world, and we should have respect for people's religious feelings. At the same time it's wise to be aware of how it can be used negatively.

通 訳

⑤ **Religion**
地下鉄サリン事件（平成9年）

オウム真理教	Aum Shinrikyo
「松本サリン事件」（1994年6月27日）	the Matsumoto Sarin gas attack
新興宗教団体	cult religious organisation
ヨガ道場	yoga training hall
住民が訴訟を起こす	local residents file a lawsuit
松本地方裁判所	Matsumoto district court
裁判官官舎	official residence of judges
サリンを撒く	scatter sarin gas
犠牲となる	become a casualty
「地下鉄サリン事件」（1995年3月20日）	Subway Sarin Attack
出勤時間	rush hour
吸引する	inhale
駅員	station staff
教祖	founder of the organisation
高学歴	highly-educated
入信する	become a follower
大規模に及ぶ	far-reaching
そこはかとない不安	vague anxiety
充満する	be filled with
「生きづらさ」	'difficulty in one's life'
負の遺産	negative legacy
secularization	世俗化
fundamentalism	原理主義
cult activity	カルト的活動
religious extremism	宗教過激派
9/11 attacks of 2001	9/11同時多発テロ
Islamic extremist group Al-Qaeda	イスラム過激派組織アルカイダ
Muslims	イスラム教徒
offshoot	枝分かれ
'new religions'	新興宗教
genuine	伝統的な
charismatic	カリスマ的
brainwashing	洗脳
Scientology	サイエントロジー
pros and cons	賛否両論
ex-members	元信者
crucial	とても重要である

5-0　Moderator 1

平成という時代は、宗教の世俗化、原理主義、そしてカルト的活動が動きを見せるなど、宗教に関してとても興味深い時代でした。それではいくつか例を見てみましょう。

5-1　Japanese Speaker 1

In June 1994, Aum Shinrikyo caused the Matsumoto Sarin gas attack. Aum Shinrikyo was a cult religious organisation; local residents filed a lawsuit against it in the 1990s, as the cult group attempted to establish a facility in Matsumoto City, Nagano Prefecture while they were opening yoga training halls across the country. As a response to this legal action, Aum Shinrikyo scattered sarin gas in the official residence of judges of the Matsumoto district court. As a result, 8 people, including students and office workers, became casualties.

5-2　Japanese Speaker 2

In the following year, 1995, on March 20, Aum Shinrikyo caused the Subway Sarin Attack on the Tokyo subway system. Sarin gas was released inside an underground train during rush hour. Those who inhaled the gas fell down one after another: 13 people including passengers and station staff were killed and approximately 6000 people were injured. The incident strongly impacted Japanese society at the time. Later on, the founder of the organisation, Shoko Asahara, was arrested, and it was discovered that many highly-educated young people had become his followers.

5-3　English Speaker 1

地下鉄サリン事件は日本にとって恐ろしい出来事であったに違いありませんね。そして平成という時代において、テロリズムと宗教過激派、そしてテロリズムとカルト的活動といった、宗教と結びつく二つの傾向があったことはとても興味深いことです。皆さんもご存知だと思いますが、2001年ニューヨークで発生した9/11同時多発テロは、イスラム過激派組織アルカイダがワールド・トレード・センターを破壊しました。約3,000人の命が奪われ、約6,000人が負傷しました。残念なことに、この事件は今日まで続く、一般的なイスラム教徒に対するいわれのない否定的なイメージを生み出してしまいました。

5-4 English Speaker 2

過激主義によって主要な宗教が枝分かれしたことに加え、平成の時代ではその多くがカルト宗教として知られる、新興宗教の増加がみられました。伝統的な宗教とカルト宗教の違いはどのように見分けられるのでしょうか。まず、カルト宗教では入信、または昇進に対し、金銭の支払いが求められます。次に、ほとんどの場合、カルト宗教にはカリスマ的指導者がいます。更には、入信者を簡単に脱退させず、思考を鈍らせるための洗脳を行います。オウム真理教はこの時代に出現した代表的なカルト宗教団体でした。欧米ではサイエントロジーというカルト宗教があり、この宗教には俳優のトム・クルーズのような有名人たちも入信しています。

5-5 Japanese Speaker 3

What could Aum's purpose have been in causing such a far-reaching horrible incident? At the time, Japanese society was filled with vague anxiety after the collapse of the Bubble Economy. Therefore, Aum Shinrikyo might have had some kind of attraction for people. The reason why many young people came to believe in Aum could be explained by the background factors of having grown up in a Japanese society in which the Bubble and its collapse left a negative legacy and 'difficulty in people's lives'.

5-6 English Speaker 3

平成の後半には、インターネットとソーシャルメディアの普及によって、宗教過激主義とカルト的活動に対する賛否両論がもたらされました。例えば、1990年代の後半にサイエントロジーの人気が衰えましたが、これは元信者らが、自分たちがした嫌な経験をネット上で簡単に共有でき、人々がカルト宗教の危険性について知ることが可能となったためです。その一方で、ソーシャルメディアはカルト宗教団体やテロ団体が自身を宣伝したり、また新たな信者らと連絡することをより容易に行えるようにもなっています。ですから、特に若者がネット上で見た情報を批判的に考えることがとても重要なのです。

5-7 Moderator 2

宗教は世界の多くの地域で話しづらい話題ではありますが、私たちは人々の宗教感を尊重しなければなりません。それと同時に、宗教がどのように悪用されうるかという点にも意識を向ける事が大切です。

Politics

ポピュリズム政治（大衆迎合主義）と外交

6-0 Moderator 1

The latter part of the Heisei era has been <u>characterized</u> by a boom in a particular type of politics: '<u>populism</u>'. So, what is populism, and what effect might it have on our societies?

(通 訳)

6-1 English Speaker 1

The word 'populism' has been used since the 19th century to describe political <u>ideologies</u> that emphasize the views of 'the people', or regular citizens, in contrast to 'the elite', which usually means wealthy and powerful people and career politicians. There have been both <u>left-wing</u> and <u>right-wing</u> populist groups; a common point is that they are often led by a <u>charismatic figure</u> who claims to '<u>speak for the people</u>'. Of course ordinary people should have their views represented in politics; but, as we'll see, populism can also have some negative effects.

(通 訳)

6-2 English Speaker 2

In the last few years there has been a trend of right-wing populism in Europe and the U.S.A. Leaders like <u>Donald Trump</u> claim to be protecting the needs of their citizens and paying attention to the problems of ordinary people. However, they tend to focus in particular on the dangers of <u>immigration</u> and <u>minority groups</u>, which has led to criticism that 'the people' for them only means white people. Therefore, populism is sometimes misunderstood as a <u>racist ideology</u>, and a <u>factor</u> in problems from <u>the U.K.'s Brexit</u> to the current immigrant <u>human rights crisis</u> at <u>the U.S. border</u>.

(通 訳)

6-3 Japanese Speaker 1

日本では、平成の30年間で首相が17人誕生しています。平均すると2年にも満たない<u>在任期間</u>です。平成が始まった1989年の5月、<u>自民党</u>がまとめた「<u>政治改革大綱</u>」の中で、「今、日本の政治は大きな<u>岐路に立た</u>されている」と語られました。その後、<u>政権交代</u>が起こりやすくなるようにと、1996年に<u>小選挙区制</u>と<u>比例代表制</u>が導入されました。

(通 訳)

6 -4　Japanese Speaker 2

また外交面では、日本経済がバブル崩壊後の低迷期により、中国が急速に発展し、以来、日本の世論は保守化していきます。2010年には中国の GDP が日本を追い越したため、中国の自信の強まりと共に尖閣諸島や歴史問題などで日本に対して強く要請を示したことも、日本国内のナショナリズムの高まりを促進しました。中国、韓国、そして北朝鮮等の近隣諸国との緊張関係は、残念ながら、令和時代に入った今現在も続いています。

(通　訳)

6 -5　English Speaker 3

So we can see that the idea of populism itself ought to be something we give careful consideration. It is certainly true that many countries face the problem of a power and wealth gap, in which a small number of people with power and influence make decisions without referring to the welfare of ordinary people. This is what populism claims to want to fix. However, in reality populism is often used to discourage people from thinking critically by appealing to their emotions instead of their logic, and this can have very damaging effects.

(通　訳)

6 -6　Japanese Speaker 3

日本でも2001年以降、当時の小泉純一郎首相による庶民的な政治スタイルが国民の高い内閣支持率によって人気を上げ、ポピュリズム政治が話題になりました。しかしその支持率の高さは、バブル崩壊後の「失われた10年」の喪失感が社会に漂っていたためとも言われています。また、今年の7月に行われた参議院選挙で、左派ポピュリズム政党の「れいわ新選組」が誕生しました。この政党は幅広い層の支持者を獲得し、今も話題を呼んでいます。

(通　訳)

6 -7　Moderator 2

Populism is on the rise around the world, and the way in which we handle it will influence the character of the Reiwa era to come.

(通　訳)

⑥ **Politics**
ポピュリズム政治（大衆迎合主義）と外交

characterize	特徴付ける
populism	ポピュリズム
ideologies	思想
left-wing	左派
right-wing	右派
charismatic figure	カリスマ的人物
'speak for the people'	人々の為に声を挙げる
Donald Trump (1946-)	ドナルド・トランプ大統領
immigration	移民
minority groups	少数派
racist ideology	人種差別的な思想
factor (n.)	要因
U.K.'s Brexit	イギリスの EU 離脱
human rights crisis	人権危機
U.S. border	アメリカ国境
power and wealth gap	権力や富の格差

在任	administration
自民党	Liberal Democratic Party (LDP)
政治改革大綱（1989年）	general principle of political reform
岐路に立つ	stand at a crossroads
政権交代	political change
小選挙区制	single-seat constituency system
比例代表制	comparative representation system
外交面	diplomatic field
低迷期	slump (n.)
保守化する	become more conservative
追い越す	overtake
尖閣諸島	Senkaku Islands
歴史問題	historical matters
要請	demand (n.)
ナショナリズムの高まり	rise of nationalism
促進する	accelerate
北朝鮮	North Korea
緊張関係	tense relationship
小泉純一郎（1942-）	prime minister Junichiro Koizumi
庶民的な政治スタイル	political style aimed at citizens
支持率	rate of support
「失われた10年」	'lost decade'
喪失感	feeling of loss
漂う	float (v.)
参議院選挙	election of the Upper House
幅広い層の支持者	wide range of supporters
話題を呼ぶ	catching people's attention

6-0   Moderator 1

平成の後半はポピュリズムという政治体系の流行によって特徴付けられます。それでは、ポピュリズムとは何なのか、そしてポピュリズムは私たちの社会にどのような影響をもたらすのでしょうか。

6-1   English Speaker 1

ポピュリズムという言葉は19世紀から、富裕層や権力者、また政治家であるエリート層とは対照的に、一般層の人々の見解を強調する政治思想を表す用語として使われています。左派と右派のポピュリズム政党があり、両者の共通点は、人々の為に声を挙げていると主張するカリスマ的人物が存在することです。もちろん、一般の人々も自身の政治に対する意見を持つべきです。しかし、ポピュリズムには負の影響も在るので、その点について見てみましょう。

6-2   English Speaker 2

ここ数年は、ヨーロッパとアメリカでは右派のポピュリズムが流行しています。ドナルド・トランプ大統領のように、国民が必要とするものを守り、人々が抱える問題に耳を傾けると主張する指導者がいます。しかしながら、彼のような人物たちは特に移民や少数派の人々の危険性に焦点を当てる傾向があり、彼らの指す人々とは白色人種のみを意味することで、批判を受けています。したがって、ポピュリズムは時に人種差別的な思想であると誤解を受けるのです。また、これはイギリスのEU離脱から、アメリカ国境で発生している移民の人権危機にわたる問題の要因でもあるのです。

6-3   Japanese Speaker 1

In Japan, 17 prime ministers and their administrations were inaugurated over the 30 years of the Heisei era. Each of the administrations lasted for less than two years on average. In May 1989, when the Heisei era began, under the general principle of political reform proposed by the Liberal Democratic Party (LDP) it was claimed that Japanese politics was standing at a crossroads. After that, in order to make it easier for political change to occur, a single-seat constituency system and comparative representation system were introduced to the election in 1996.

6-4   Japanese Speaker 2

Also, in the diplomatic field, public opinion in Japan had been becoming more conservative since the development of China brought on by the slump in the Japanese economy after the collapse of the Bubble Economy. The rise of nationalism in Japan was accelerated because China's GDP overtook Japan's in 2010, as well as due to China's increasing confidence and their strong demands based on the Senkaku Islands and historical matters. Japan's tense relationships with neighbouring countries such as China, South Korea and North Korea is unfortunately continuing even now we've entered the Reiwa era.

6-5　English Speaker 3

ですから、ポピュリズムという考え方自体、注意深く考えなければいけません。多くの国々が権力や富の格差の問題を抱えていますが、そこでは、一握りの権力者や影響力のある人々が一般の人々の福祉に言及することなく、決断を下しています。これは、ポピュリズムにおいて修復すべき点と主張しています。しかし実際には、人々に論理よりも感情に訴えかけることで、ポピュリズムは人々を批判的思考から遠ざけています。その様な使われ方こそが、ポピュリズムの弊害と言えるでしょう。

6-6　Japanese Speaker 3

Since 2001, populism politics caught on in Japan too. This was because the political style aimed at citizens by the then prime minister, Junichiro Koizumi, raised his popularity with a high rate of support. However, it is also said that the height of the support rate was due to the feeling of loss from 'the lost decade' after the collapse of the Bubble Economy that was floating around society. Furthermore, at the election of the Upper house in July this year, a left-wing populist party, 'Reiwa Shinsengumi', was established. The political party has a wide range of supporters and is still catching people's attention now.

6-7　Moderator 2

ポピュリズムは世界中で広がっており、私たちがポピュリズムをどのように扱うのかが来る令和の時代を決定づけるでしょう。

Natural Disasters

東日本大震災（2011年3月11日）

Keywords

阪神・淡路大震災（1995年1月17日）
東日本大震災（2011年3月11日）
最大級の
衝撃的な映像
耐震基準
襲来する
悲劇をもたらす
東京電力福島第一原子力発電所
原発の安全神話
水素爆発
放射性物質
放出する
拡散
追われる
移住する
全容
解明する
メルケル首相（1954-）
文在寅大統領（1953-）
白紙に戻す
原発政策
全面的に
見直す
エネルギー政策

Haiti earthquake (2010)
Hurricane Katrina (2005)
billions of dollars
Hurricane Maria (2017)
U.S. colony of Puerto Rico
volcanic eruption
withstand earthquakes
at-risk areas
fault lines
human spirit
infrastructure
vital

7 -0　Moderator 1

Natural disasters have affected humans deeply throughout history, and Japan in particular is well prepared for them. But some disasters are huge enough to impact an entire country and beyond.

(通 訳)

7 -1　Japanese Speaker 1

平成は、1995年の阪神・淡路大震災、そして2011年の東日本大震災など、戦後最大級の災害が日本を襲った時代でもありました。阪神・淡路大震災が発生したのは1月17日、午前5時46分という早朝でした。テレビで流れる完全に崩壊された高速道路の光景は、衝撃的な映像として今でも多くの人々の記憶に残っていると思います。命を失った人々は6,400人以上に上り、この震災により全国の耐震基準が見直されることになります。

(通 訳)

7 -2　Japanese Speaker 2

東日本大震災では、最大で20メートルを超える大津波が襲来し、15,000人以上の命を奪いました。またこの震災では、もう一つの悲劇をもたらします。東京電力福島第一原子力発電所の事故です。原発の安全神話は一瞬にして崩れ去ったのです。水素爆発により大量の放射性物質が大気中に放出され、その拡散範囲は第一原発から遠く離れたここ中部地方にまで及んだと言われています。そして、原発事故により、多くの人々が故郷を追われ、全国各地に移住を強いられました。

(通 訳)

7 -3　English Speaker 1

Japan isn't the only country to suffer from natural disasters during this era. One of the worst earthquakes was the one that struck Haiti in 2010, making buildings collapse and killing over 200,000 people. Hurricanes were also severe; the most famous was Hurricane Katrina, which hit the city of New Orleans in the USA in 2005, killing almost 2,000 and causing billions of dollars in damage. This was followed by Hurricane Maria in 2017, which caused huge damage to the U.S. colony of Puerto Rico.

(通 訳)

7-4 English Speaker 2

During the Heisei era we have come to learn more about natural disasters. Technology has advanced, making it possible to predict earthquakes and volcanic eruptions more accurately. Further, developments in construction mean we can create buildings that can withstand earthquakes in at-risk areas. Japan now has strict building laws to help keep people safe, and cities like Nagoya that lie on fault lines have detailed plans to help prepare for major earthquakes. However, it's also true that there are still many problems regarding how we deal with natural disasters.

通 訳

7-5 Japanese Speaker 3

震災から8年以上経た現在も、第一原発事故の全容は未だ解明されていません。しかしこの事故をきっかけに、ドイツのメルケル首相は2020年末までにすべての原発を安全に停止する方針を決めました。アジアでも韓国の文在寅大統領が新規の原発建設を白紙に戻すなど、原発政策を全面的に見直す方針を明らかにしました。この原発事故は、世界のエネルギー政策にまで大きな影響を与えたのです。

通 訳

7-6 English Speaker 3

Natural disasters in recent years have shown us the strength of the human spirit and the cooperation of communities. At the same time, the Haiti earthquake and Hurricanes Katrina and Maria have revealed problems with how we handle these disasters. In Haiti insufficient building laws increased the damage, and limited infrastructure meant it was difficult to get rescuers and supplies to victims. After Katrina the U.S. government was criticized for being slow to respond, and this happened again after Maria. So even in developed countries we still have many improvements to make.

通 訳

7-7 Moderator 2

With more and more people living in urban areas, it's vital that we learn to prepare properly for natural disasters as we go forward into the Reiwa era.

通 訳

⑦ Natural Disasters
東日本大震災（2011年3月11日）

阪神・淡路大震災（1995年1月17日）	Great Hanshin-Awaji earthquake
東日本大震災（2011年3月11日）	Great East Japan earthquake
最大級の	on the largest scale
衝撃的な映像	a shocking image
耐震基準	building durability standards
襲来する	engulf
悲劇をもたらす	bring tragedy
東京電力福島第一原子力発電所	TEPCO's Fukushima No.1 nuclear power plant
原発の安全神話	false belief in the safety of nuclear plants
水素爆発	hydrogen explosion
放射性物質	radioactive substance
放出する	release
拡散	diffuse (v.)
追われる	force to leave
移住する	relocate
全容	full story
解明する	uncover
メルケル首相（1954-）	Chancellor Angela Merkel
文在寅大統領（1953-）	President Moon Jae-in
白紙に戻す	call off
原発政策	policy regarding nuclear power plants
全面的に	entirely
見直す	revise
エネルギー政策	energy consumption policy
Haiti earthquake (2010)	ハイチ大地震
Hurricane Katrina (2005)	ハリケーン・カトリーナ
billions of dollars	何十億ドル
Hurricane Maria (2017)	ハリケーン・マリア
U.S. colony of Puerto Rico	アメリカ自治区であるプエルトリコ
volcanic eruption	火山の噴火
withstand earthquakes	耐震の
at-risk areas	被災の可能性のある地域
fault lines	活断層
human spirit	人間の精神力
infrastructure	インフラ
vital	重要である

Moderator 1

自然災害は人類の歴史の中で深刻な影響を与えてきました。特に日本は自然災害に対しての防災意識は高いです。それでも災害の中には国全体どころかそれ以上の影響を与えうる巨大な災害もあります。

7-1

Japanese Speaker 1

The Heisei era was a time in which natural disasters hit Japan <u>on the largest scale</u>, such as <u>the Great Hanshin-Awaji earthquake</u> in 1995 and <u>Great East Japan earthquake</u> in 2011. The Great Hanshin-Awaji earthquake occurred at 5:46 am on January 17. The scene of completely collapsed highways broadcast on television still remains in many people's memories as <u>a shocking image</u>. The number of people killed by the earthquake rose to over 6,400, which triggered revisions of <u>building durability standards</u> in Japan to improve safety.

7-2

Japanese Speaker 2

After the Great East Japan earthquake, a tsunami of over 20 meters <u>engulfed</u> the land and claimed over 15,000 lives. The natural disaster <u>brought</u> another <u>tragedy</u>, which was the incident involving TEPCO's Fukushima No.1 nuclear <u>power plant</u>. People's <u>false belief in the safety of nuclear plants</u> was destroyed in a moment by the incident. A <u>hydrogen explosion</u> released radioactive <u>substances</u> into the air and <u>diffused</u> them over a wide area, reaching even as far as the Chubu region here, which is quite a distance from Fukushima. In addition to this, the TEPCO incident <u>forced locals to leave</u> their hometown and <u>relocate</u> elsewhere in Japan.

7-3

English Speaker 1

この平成の時代に自然災害に苦しめられた国は日本だけではありません。最も恐ろしかった地震の一つは、2010年ハイチを襲った地震で、建物を倒壊させ、20万人もの人々の命を奪いました。ハリケーンもまた甚大な被害を及ぼし、最も良く知られているハリケーンは2005年にアメリカのニューオーリンズ州の街を襲った<u>ハリケーン・カトリーナ</u>でした。この災害では、およそ2000人の命を奪い、<u>何十億ドル</u>もの被害を出しました。これに続く2017年の<u>ハリケーン・マリア</u>で、<u>アメリカ自治区である</u>プエルトリコに深刻な被害を与えました。

7-4   English Speaker 2

平成では、私たちは自然災害について、より多くのことを学びました。科学技術が進化し、地震と火山の噴火をより正確に予知できるようになりました。さらに、建築分野における進歩と言えば、被災の可能性のある地域に、耐震の建物を建築することが可能になりました。日本には厳しい建築基準法があり、これは人々の安全に一役買っています。また、名古屋のような活断層上の都市では、巨大地震に備えた周到な計画が立てられています。しかしながら、どのように自然災害に対処するかは、未だ数多くの問題が残されていることも確かです。

7-5   Japanese Speaker 3

Even though it has been more than eight years since the Great East Japan earthquake, the <u>full story</u> of the Fukushima I nuclear power plant has not yet been <u>uncovered</u>. However, taking the incident as an opportunity, <u>the German chancellor Angela Merkel</u> determined on a policy to safely suspend every one of their nuclear power plants until the end of 2020. Also, in Asia, <u>the South Korean president Moon Jae-in</u> revealed his attitude to <u>entirely</u> <u>revise</u> his <u>policy regarding nuclear power plants</u>, <u>calling off</u> the establishment of a new plant. This nuclear power plant mishap massively influenced the world's <u>energy consumption policy</u>.

7-6   English Speaker 3

近年の自然災害は私たちに人間の精神力の強さとコミュニティーの協力体制を示してくれました。それと同時に、ハイチ大地震とハリケーンカトリーナやハリケーンマリアでは私たちの自然災害に対する対処法についての問題点が明らかになりました。ハイチでは不十分な建築基準法が被害を拡大し、インフラが限られていたため救助と救援物資を被災者に届けることが困難になりました。ハリケーン・カトリーナの後、アメリカ政府による対応の遅れが批判され、ハリケーン・マリアの後も同じことが起こりました。すなわち、先進諸国においてもまだまだ改善の余地はあるのです。

7-7   Moderator 2

都市部で生活する人々がますます増えており、これからの令和の時代においては自然災害に対して適切な備えを整えていくことがとても重要です。

Media

メディアの役割

Keywords

cannot be overestimated	相次ぐ
state-sponsored television	人権やプライバシーの侵害
bias	権力からの圧力
interpret	社会に蔓延する
advent	「ポスト真実」
trustworthy	第一通報者
the Collins Dictionary	河野義行（1950-）
Word of the Year	長野県警
new media	容疑者扱いにされる
Twitter	罷免する
populist politician	世間
Islamic extremist group	想像を絶する
9/11	屈辱
	元オウム幹部
	死刑執行
	情報伝達の進歩
	映像
	地球の隅々まで
	利便性
	敏感でいる
	拘束する
	フリージャーナリスト
	安田順平（1974-）
	武装集団
	解放する
	「自己責任論」
	議論を呼ぶ
	使命
	称える

8-0 Moderator 1

In every topic we've considered so far today, the role of media <u>cannot be overestimated</u>. Media changed a lot in the Heisei era and our way of dealing with it must change too.

> 通 訳

8-1 English Speaker 1

Prior to the Heisei era, when people thought of media they usually meant 'mass media': commercial and <u>state-sponsored television</u>, radio, newspapers, magazines, and so on. There were relatively few places where you could get information. So, even though it was understood that different newspapers or TV stations could hold different political <u>biases</u>, people generally trusted the facts given by the media. Of course, it was useful to be able to critically <u>interpret</u> these facts for yourself but compared to today it wasn't essential.

> 通 訳

8-2 English Speaker 2

In the 1990s, however, the <u>advent</u> of the Internet and then social media meant that hundreds, even thousands of information sources became available. Because of this it has become difficult for people to understand what information is <u>trustworthy</u>. We can now find information that hasn't been checked by experts or editors; it's for this reason that the term 'fake news' became <u>the Collins Dictionary</u>'s <u>Word of the Year</u> in 2017. So, in order to judge the reliability of these sources we need to be skilled critical thinkers.

> 通 訳

8-3 Japanese Speaker 1

平成は大きな事件や災害が<u>相次ぎ</u>、メディアの役割が改めて問われる時代でした。<u>人権や</u> <u>プライバシーの侵害</u>、権力からの<u>圧力</u>、そしてインターネットとスマートフォンによって 誰もが発信可能になり、フェイクニュースという恐ろしい情報源も<u>社会</u>に<u>蔓延する</u>ように なりました。今や私たちは、真実が重要でも適切でもなくなった「<u>ポスト真実</u>」の時代に 生きています。

> 通 訳

8-4 Japanese Speaker 2

先にも述べた1994年に起った「松本サリン事件」ですが、第一通報者で被害者でもあった河野義行さんが長野県警から約一年間、容疑者扱いにされました。翌年の1995年に「地下鉄サリン事件」が起きたことにより、河野さんは罷免され、警察、メディア各社は謝罪しました。世間から想像を絶する屈辱を経験しながらも、河野さんは元オウム幹部の死刑執行に対して最後まで反対した方です。

通 訳

8-5 English Speaker 3

Despite being more difficult to interpret, media is as influential as ever. Both mass media and new media can affect how we think about social issues, and even how we act. For example, the use of Twitter to speak directly to citizens has been used effectively by populist politicians to gain support for their policies. Further, the way mass media represented Islamic extremist groups during 9/11 has had a negative effect on the image of ordinary Muslims in the West.

通 訳

8-6 Japanese Speaker 3

今や、情報伝達の進歩によって、様々な出来事は映像と共に地球の隅々まで送り届けられる時代になりました。同時に、その利便性に対して、私たちは敏感でなくてはなりません。2018年10月、シリアで拘束されていたフリージャーナリストの安田順平さんが武装集団から解放されました。この出来事をめぐり、日本では「自己責任論」が飛び交い、議論を呼びます。一方フランスでは、「彼のような人がいなければ、我々はシリアの真実を知ることができない」と、安田さんのジャーナリストとしての使命が称えられました。

通 訳

8-7 Moderator 2

We have more of a role in the use of media than ever before; we even make our own media through Twitter, Instagram, etc. So it's essential that we learn to understand it.

通 訳

8 Media
メディアの役割

cannot be overestimated	計り知れない
state-sponsored television	国営テレビ放送
bias	偏見
interpret	解釈する
advent	出現する
trustworthy	信頼に値する
the Collins Dictionary	コリンズ英語辞書
Word of the Year	流行語大賞
new media	新しいメディア
Twitter	ツイッター
populist politician	ポピュリズム政治家
Islamic extremist group	イスラム過激派組織
9/11	9/11同時多発テロ事件

相次ぐ	one after another
人権やプライバシーの侵害	infringements of human rights and privacy
権力からの圧力	oppression by authorities
社会に蔓延する	run rampant in society
「ポスト真実」	'post-truth'
第一通報者	the first person who notified the police
河野義行（1950-）	Yoshiyuki Kono
長野県警	Nagano prefectural police
容疑者扱いにされる	be treated as a suspect
罷免する	discharge (v.)
世間	public (n.)
想像を絶する	unimaginable
屈辱	humiliation
元オウム幹部	former Aum leaders
死刑執行	execution
情報伝達の進歩	progress of information transmission
映像	image
地球の隅々まで	every corner of the planet
利便性	convenience
敏感でいる	stay alert
拘束する	detain
フリージャーナリスト	freelance journalist
安田順平（1974-）	Junpei Yasuda
武装集団	armed group
解放する	release (v.)
「自己責任論」	arguments about 'self-responsibility'
議論を呼ぶ	controversial
使命	mission
称える	praise

Moderator 1

今日、これまで話してきたどのトピックにおいても、メディアの役割は<u>計りしれません</u>。平成の時代はメディアによって大きく変化しました。同時に、私たちのメディアとの付き合い方も変えていくべきです。

8 -1

English Speaker 1

平成以前では、メディアと言えば、広告、<u>国営テレビ放送</u>、ラジオ、新聞や雑誌といったマスメディアを意味していました。情報源は比較的限られていました。なので、それぞれの新聞社やテレビ局によって異なった政治的偏見があったのは分かっていましたが、人々はメディアから与えられた事実を信じていました。もちろん、このようにメディアから与えられた事実は、自分自身で批判的に<u>解釈する</u>ことはできましたが、今日ほどの重要性はありませんでした。

8 -2

English Speaker 2

しかしながら、1990年代には、インターネットとその後のソーシャルメディアの<u>出現</u>で何百、何千もの情報源が入手可能となりました。これによって、人々がどの情報が<u>信頼に値する</u>のかを判断することがより困難なものとなりました。今日、専門家や編集者が確認しないままの情報が出回っています。そのため、2017年<u>コリンズ英語辞書の流行語大賞</u>に「フェイクニュース」が選ばれました。このような理由から、情報源の信頼性を判断するために、私たちは批判的思考力を高めていく必要があります。

8 -3

Japanese Speaker 1

The Heisei era was a time in which major incidents and natural disasters happened <u>one after another</u>, and the role of media was questioned once again. With <u>infringements of human rights and privacy</u>, <u>oppression by authorities</u>, and the Internet and smartphones enabling anyone to transmit information, worrying information sources known as fake news <u>ran rampant in society</u>. We are currently living in a '<u>post-truth</u>' period where the truth has become neither important nor appropriate.

8 -4

Japanese Speaker 2

As I mentioned before, regarding the Matsumoto sarin gas attack that occurred in 1994, <u>Yoshiyuki Kono</u> was <u>the first person who notified the police</u>, and was also one of the victims. However, he <u>was treated as a suspect</u> by <u>the Nagano prefectural police</u> for approximately one year. In the following year, 1995, as a result of the subway gas attack, Mr. Kono was <u>discharged</u> and received an apology from the police and mass media. Even though he experienced <u>unimaginable public humiliation</u>, he opposed the <u>executions</u> of <u>the former Aum leaders</u> until the last moment.

8-5　　English Speaker 3

情報の解釈が非常に困難な中であっても、依然としてメディアは今まで以上に影響力を持つようになりました。マスメディアと<u>新しいメディア</u>の両方が私たちの社会問題への考え方や、私たちの行動にまで影響を及ぼしています。例を挙げると、<u>ポピュリズム政治家</u>は、自分たちの政策への支持を獲得するために、市民に直接語り掛けるなど、効果的に<u>Twitter</u>を利用してきました。さらに、<u>9/11同時多発テロ事件</u>における<u>イスラム過激派組織</u>についての報道の仕方が原因で、西側諸国における一般のイスラム教徒の印象までも悪くしてしまいました。

8-6　　Japanese Speaker 3

The <u>progress of information transmission</u> in this period has made it possible for us to transmit information about various incidents along with <u>images</u> to <u>every corner of the planet</u>. At the same time, we have to <u>stay alert</u> regarding its <u>convenience</u>. In October 2018, <u>Junpei Yasuda</u>, <u>a freelance journalist</u> who had been <u>detained</u> in Syria, was <u>released</u> from the custody of <u>an armed group</u>. <u>Controversial</u> <u>arguments</u> about 'self-responsibility' spread around Japan due to this event. In France, on the other hand, his <u>mission</u> as a journalist was <u>praised</u> by people claiming that "if people like him did not exist, we would not be able to know the truth about Syria."

8-7　　Moderator 2

メディアを使う際、私たちの役割も増えましたね。Twitter、Instagram などを通して個人のメディアを作ることもできます。ですから、メディアを理解して学ぶことが大切です。

9
Literature
国境を超える文学とその役割

Keywords

日本文学研究者	diplomacy
翻訳者	conflict
ドナルド・キーン（1922-2019）	British-Indian
過言ではない	Salman Rushdie (1947-)
近現代	"The Satanic Verses"
学者	atheist
古典文学	explore
再認識	depiction
功績 contribution	prophet Muhammad
日本へ帰化する	controversy
表明	spiritual leader
反響を呼ぶ	*fatwa*
日米関係	break off diplomatic relations
雲行きが怪しくなる	assassination attempt
『源氏物語』	chaos
英訳書	riot (n.)
東洋文学者	freedom of expression
アーサー・ウェイリー（1889-1966）	to be knighted
海軍の情報将校	regardless of
従軍する	web comic
捕虜になる	Cho Nam-ju (1982-)
恥じて死を求める	bestselling
日本再建	"Kim Ji-Young, Born in 1982"
谷崎潤一郎（1886-1965）	sexism
川端康成（1899-1972）	
三島由紀夫（1925-1970）	
交友を持つ	
損なわれる	
真剣に捉える	
対話	
訴える	

9-0 Moderator 1

Reading can both entertain and educate us; but literature also has a huge role to play in politics, diplomacy, conflict, and peace.

(通 訳)

9-1 Japanese Speaker 1

2019年2月、アメリカ生まれの日本文学研究者で翻訳者でもあるドナルド・キーン先生が、96歳で亡くなりました。平成とともに去っていかれたといっても過言ではありません。キーン氏は『万葉集』から近現代の日本文学まで幅広く海外へ紹介した学者であり、日本人にも古典文学の魅力を再確認させた功績が称えられています。また、東日本大震災直後に日本へ帰化することを表明し、大きな反響を呼んだ方でもありました。

(通 訳)

9-2 Japanese Speaker 2

日米関係の雲行きが怪しくなっていた1940年、当時18歳だったキーン氏はニューヨークの書店で『源氏物語』の英訳書を手にし、そこで初めて日本文学と出会いました。イギリス人の東洋文学者であるアーサー・ウェイリーによる英訳文の素晴らしさに強く惹かれたといいます。キーン氏は戦時中、海軍の情報将校として沖縄などに従軍しました。そこで、捕虜になったことを恥じて死を求める日本兵を目にし、キーン氏は兵士たちに「日本の再建のために生きるべきだ」と説得しました。

(通 訳)

9-3 English Speaker 1

The U.K. also has examples of literature that has raised questions about society, and has even influenced the relationship between nations. In 1988, one year before Heisei began, a British-Indian author named Salman Rushdie published a novel titled "The Satanic Verses". Rushdie was raised Muslim and later became an atheist, but he was very interested in exploring religion and social issues. By 1989, however, his novel and its depiction of the prophet Muhammad had caused huge controversy in the Muslim world.

(通 訳)

9-4　English Speaker 2

The book was banned in 13 countries, and in February 1989 the spiritual leader of Iran issued an official *fatwā* against him. Because of this the U.K. and Iran broke off diplomatic relations until 1998, and Rushdie had to live under police protection. The *fatwā* led to violence around the world, with assassination attempts on Rushdie and riots protesting the book in which people died. From one novel came years of chaos, but also discussions about religion and freedom of expression; and in 2007 Rushdie was knighted by the U.K. for his services to literature.

(通　訳)

9-5　Japanese Speaker 3

キーン氏は戦後、谷崎潤一郎、川端康成、三島由紀夫などの日本を代表する作家たちとも交友を持ちました。近年では、日本が戦後築き上げてきた平和が損なわれるのではないかと強く懸念していたと言います。そのため、日本が平和であるためには、日本人は日本文学をもっと真剣に捉えないといけないと何度も語っています。また、立場や考え方が違っても、人間は対話によって必ず解決策に到達できると、言葉の持つ力を周囲の人々に訴え続けました。

(通　訳)

9-6　English Speaker 3

Regardless of the spread of new types of media like YouTube videos and web comics, literature still has a key place in our society: to teach us, make us think, and of course entertain us. For example, in 2016 a South Korean writer, Cho Nam-ju, published a bestselling novel titled "Kim Ji-Young, Born in 1982"; the book is about the everyday sexism experienced by an ordinary woman, and has led to public debate about the place of feminism in Korea. Books will always engage with social problems and will therefore cause controversy.

(通　訳)

9-7　Moderator 2

There are various roles literature can play in our lives; but we should never forget to think about what we read with an open mind.

(通　訳)

9 Literature
国境を超える文学とその役割

日本文学研究者	researcher of Japanese literature
翻訳者	translator
ドナルド・キーン（1922-2019）	Donald Lawrence Keene
過言ではない	would not be an exaggeration
近現代	modern
学者	scholar
古典文学	classic literature
再認識	recapture
功績	contribution
日本へ帰化する	be naturalised as a Japanese citizen
表明	announcement
反響を呼ぶ	evoke a huge reaction
日米関係	Japan-U.S. relations
雲行きが怪しくなる	be not at a high point
『源氏物語』	"The Tale of Genji"
英訳書	English version
東洋文学者	scholar of Asian literature
アーサー・ウェイリー（1889-1966）	Arthur David Waley
海軍の情報将校	navy intelligence officer
従軍する	be deployed
捕虜になる	be captured
恥じて死を求める	ask for death out of shame
日本再建	rebuild Japan
谷崎潤一郎（1886-1965）	Junichiro Tanizaki
川端康成（1899-1972）	Yasunari Kawabata
三島由紀夫（1925-1970）	Yukio Mishima
交友を持つ	have friendships with
損なわれる	be undermined
真剣に捉える	grasp seriously
対話	dialogue
訴える	promote

diplomacy	外交
conflict	紛争
British-Indian	イギリス系インド人
Salman Rushdie (1947-)	サーマン・ラシュディー
"The Satanic Verses"	『悪魔の詩』
atheist	無神論者
explore	探求する
depiction	描写
prophet Muhammad	預言者ムハンマド
controversy	賛否両論
spiritual leader	宗教指導者
fatwa	ファトワ
break off diplomatic relations	外交関係が断絶する
assassination attempt	暗殺未遂
chaos	混乱
riot (n.)	暴動
freedom of expression	表現の自由
to be knighted	ナイトの称号が与えられる
regardless of	～にもかかわらず
web comic	ウェブ漫画
Cho Nam-ju (1982-)	チョ・ナムジュ
bestselling	ベストセラー
"Kim Ji-Young, Born in 1982"	『82年生まれ、キム・ジヨン』
sexism	性差別

9-0   **Moderator 1**

読書は私たちを楽しませてくれ、また多くのことを教えてくれます。しかし、文学自体も政治、外交、紛争、そして平和の中で大きな役割を担っているものです。

9-1   **Japanese Speaker 1**

Professor Donald Keene, a researcher of Japanese literature and translator who was born in the U.S., passed away at age 96 in February 2019. It would not be an exaggeration to say that that he took his leave along with the Heisei era. Prof. Keene was a scholar who introduced Japanese literature widely overseas, from the collection of Japanese songs called the "Man'yōshū" to modern works. His contribution to helping Japanese people recapture the attractions of classic literature has been praised. Also, his announcement that he would be naturalised as a Japanese citizen directly after the Great East Japan earthquake evoked a huge reaction from the public.

9-2   **Japanese Speaker 2**

In 1940, when Japan-U.S. relations were not at a high point, Prof. Keene encountered Japanese literature for the first time, getting hold of the English version of "The Tale of Genji" at a bookstore in New York when he was 18. It's said that he was strongly attracted by the excellent English translation of the British scholar of Asian literature, Arthur Waley. During the War, Keene was deployed as a navy intelligence officer in Okinawa, etc. Seeing captured Japanese soldiers ask for death out of shame, he persuaded them that they "should live in order to rebuild Japan".

9-3   **English Speaker 1**

イギリスにもまた文学が社会に疑問を投げかけ、他国との関係に影響をもたらした例があります。平成が始まる一年前の1988年には、イギリス系インド人作家であるサーマン・ラシュディーが『悪魔の詩』という小説を出版しました。ラシュディー氏はイスラム教徒として生まれ、後に無神論者となりましたが、彼は宗教と社会問題を探求することにとても熱意のある人物であったのです。しかしながら、1989年に至るまで、彼の小説と預言者ムハンマドの描写はイスラム教世界で激しい賛否両論が起きていました。

9-4   **English Speaker 2**

その本は13か国で禁止され、1989年の2月にはイランの宗教指導者が彼に対してイスラム法令である「ファトワ」を発令しました。このことが原因でイギリスとイランの外交関係は1998年まで断絶したのです。ラシュディーは警察の保護下に置かれて生活しなければなりませんでした。そのファトワは世界中に暴力を引き起こし、ラシュディー氏への暗殺未遂や、本の抗議を行う暴動では死者が出ました。一冊の小説から何年にもわたる混乱が起こりましたが、宗教と表現の自由についての議論が巻き起こり、2007年にラシュディーは文学へ貢献したとしてイギリスよりナイトの称号が与えられました。

9-5 Japanese Speaker 3

Mr Keene had friendships with authors representing Japan after WW2 like Junichiro Tanizaki, Yasunari Kawabata, and Yukio Mishima. It is said that in recent years he was awfully concerned that the peace the country had built in the post-war period would be undermined. Therefore, for the sake of keeping Japan at peace, he has often said that Japanese people should grasp Japanese literature more seriously. He also continuously promoted the power of words to people by insisting that human beings can definitely arrive at a solution though dialogue, even among people of different social statuses and ways of thinking.

9-6 English Speaker 3

YouTube の動画やウェブ漫画のような新しい形のメディアの普及にもかかわらず、文学は私たちの社会で重要な地位を保ち続けています。つまり、私たちは文学から学び、考え、ときには楽しむこともできます。例えば、2016年に韓国の作家であるチョ・ナムジュは『82年生まれ、キム・ジヨン』というベストセラー小説を出版しました。その書籍は一般的な女性が経験した日常的な性差別について書かれており、韓国でのフェミニズムの在り方に関して、世の中で議論を引き起こしました。本は常に社会問題と結びついており、それ故に物議を醸すものなのでしょう。

9-7 Moderator 2

私たちの生活において、文学は様々な役割を果たしていますが、私たちは開かれた心をもって読書することを忘れてはいけません。

10

Wishes for the Reiwa era

令和への願い（2019年5月1日）

Keywords

key area	描写する
acceptance	「生きづらさ」
diversity	～を振り返る
sexuality	人生の意義
authority figure	感覚を抱く
harmonious	目に見える
embrace	外的なもの
open mind	安心
weigh	内面的な要素
critical mind	意味を持つ
	社会現象
	相次ぐ
	一国主義
	勢力を増す
	傾向
	異なる他者
	相互関係を築く
	教養教育
	目まぐるしく
	希薄化する
	自分の殻から出る
	出会いを求める

10 -0   Moderator 1

The Heisei era was a time of great change, good and bad. What kind of era do we wish Reiwa to be, and what should we do to achieve it?

通 訳

10-1 English Speaker 1

Today we've discussed major trends and changes in <u>key areas</u> of the Heisei era: in technology, culture, politics, religion, and so on. In the last 30 years there has been great progress in <u>acceptance</u> of <u>diversity</u>: learning to live in peace alongside people from different cultures, with different beliefs and <u>sexualities</u>. But we've also seen that there is still discrimination from both <u>authority figures</u> and ordinary citizens that stops us becoming a truly <u>harmonious</u> world. I believe this is what we should try to solve in the new Reiwa era.

(通　訳)

10-2 English Speaker 2

One of the keywords of recent times is 'a global society', and we are all encouraged to become good global citizens. But what does this really mean? For many people globalization means the opportunity to mix with cultures around the world. Others, however, have criticized globalization because they worry it might make unique individual cultures disappear. I think being a good global citizen in the Reiwa era means actively trying to <u>embrace</u> various cultures and learn from them, while also protecting the good points of our native culture.

(通　訳)

10-3 Japanese Speaker 1

平成の日本人を<u>描写する</u>キーワードとして、「<u>生きづらさ</u>」が挙げられます。近年、平成を<u>振り返る</u>多くの書籍が出版されましたが、必ずこの用語が扱われているのです。社会で生きることがつらい、<u>人生の意義</u>がわからない、そうした<u>感覚を抱いている</u>人は今も少なくありません。ですから、政治、経済といった<u>目に見える</u>外的なものだけではなく、アイデンティティー、<u>安心</u>、支え、そして生きる意義などの<u>内面的な要素</u>が、より大きな<u>意味を持つ</u>ようになりました。

(通　訳)

Japanese Speaker 2

しかし、この「生きづらさ」という社会現象は、日本だけではなく世界各国にも及ぶものでした。海外では戦争が相次ぎ、また一国主義が勢力を増していく傾向が各地で現れたからです。では、このような社会に生きる若者に何ができるでしょうか。それは、自分とは異なる他者との出会いを恐れず、対話によって相互関係を築こうとする人間に成長することです。そのためには、大学で養われる教養教育が大きな助けになるでしょう。

通 訳

10 -5 **English Speaker 3**

As a British person who has lived in Japan during the Heisei and Reiwa eras, I often ask myself how I can use my experiences to help young people become citizens who will have a good influence on the world. I've found that the most important qualities to have are: an open mind to understand things that seem 'strange' about new cultures; a critical mind to weigh the positive and negative points of my own society and others; and a kind heart to accept all the different people around me. I hope that this can help us make the Reiwa era truly 'an era for everyone'.

通 訳

10 -6 **Japanese Speaker 3**

平成は、目まぐるしく進化する技術が私たちの生活を大きく変えた時代でした。令和に入り、AIのさらなる進化によって、「人間とは何か」が今まで以上に問われる時代となっていくでしょう。人とのつながりが希薄化している現代だからこそ、私たちは自分の殻から出て、他者との出会いを求める勇気が必要です。そして何より日本は、世界が平和を維持できるように、日本文化の本来の美しさを再発見し、それを世界に発信していく役目があります。新元号の令和は、そう私たちに教えてくれているかのようです。

通 訳

10 -7 **Moderator 2**

The final question for all of us is: how can each of us do our best, as students, teachers, and global citizens, to make our wishes for the Reiwa era come true?

通 訳

⑩ Wishes for the Reiwa era
令和への願い（2019年5月1日）

key area	重要な分野
acceptance	享受すること
diversity	多様性
sexuality	性的嗜好
authority figure	権力者
harmonious	調和のとれた
embrace	受け入れる
open mind	広い心を持つこと
weigh	比較考察する
critical mind	批判的な心

描写する	depict
「生きづらさ」	'difficulty of living'
〜を振り返る	bring back memories of
人生の意義	the meaning of one's life
感覚を抱く	feel
目に見える	visible
外的なもの	external things
安心	security
内面的な要素	internal elements
意味を持つ	become meaningful
社会現象	social phenomenon
相次ぐ	successive
一国主義	nationalism
勢力を増す	grow influence
傾向	tendency
異なる他者	different people
相互関係を築く	build mutual human connection
教養教育	liberal arts education
目まぐるしく	rapidly
希薄化する	get weaker
自分の殻から出る	come out of one's shell
出会いを求める	seek encounters

10-0　Moderator 1

平成は、良くも悪くも大きな変化が訪れた時代でした。私たちは令和の時代に何を願い、それを実現させるためには何をすべきでしょうか。

10-1　English Speaker 1

今日は平成の時代での科学技術、文化、政治、宗教といった欠かすことのできない<u>重要な分野</u>における主な傾向と変化について話し合ってきました。過去30年において、<u>多様性を享受すること</u>において大きな進歩がありました。つまり、異なる文化や信条、<u>性的嗜好</u>を持つ人々と共に仲良く生きていくことを学ぶということです。しかし一方で、<u>権力者と一般市民の双方からの差別</u>が未だにあり、真に<u>調和のとれた世界</u>となるのを妨げています。私はこの点こそが新しい令和の時代で解決すべき点であると思うのです。

10-2　English Speaker 2

近年を表す言葉の一つに「グローバル社会」というものが挙げられ、私たちは良きグローバル市民になるよう求められています。しかし、良きグローバル市民になるということは一体どういうことなのでしょうか。多くの方々にとって、グローバリゼーションとは世界中の文化と交わり合うことを意味します。しかしながら、他方では、グローバリゼーションは個々の文化の特徴がなくなってしまうかもしれないということで批判を受けています。私は良きグローバル市民になることは自分たちの文化の良い点を守りつつ、他の様々な文化を積極的に<u>受け入れ</u>、それらから学んでいくことであると思うのです。

10-3　Japanese Speaker 1

One of the keywords <u>depicting</u> Japanese people in the Heisei era is 'difficulty of living'. Many books that <u>bring back memories of</u> the Heisei era have been published in recent years which absolutely use this term. There are quite a few people who <u>feel</u> that it is painful to live in this society, do not understand <u>the meaning of their lives</u>. Because of that, not only <u>visible external things</u> such as politics and the economy, but also identity, <u>security</u>, support and the meaning of life, as <u>internal elements</u> appeared to have <u>become</u> much more <u>meaningful</u> than before.

10-4　Japanese Speaker 2

Nevertheless, this <u>social phenomenon</u> of the difficulty of living has not been limited to Japan but also affects other countries in the world. This can be seen in a worldwide <u>tendency</u> for <u>successive</u> wars and the <u>growing influence</u> of <u>nationalism</u>. So, what kind of thing can young people living in such a world do? They can grow up as a person who is not afraid of encountering <u>different people</u> and intends to <u>build mutual human connection</u> though dialogue. In order to achieve that, <u>liberal arts education</u> cultivated at university would be a big help.

10-5　English Speaker 3

平成と令和の時代を日本で生活している一人のイギリス人として、私はよく自分自身に問いかけることがあります。若者たちが世界に良い影響を与えられる市民になるためには、私はどのように自身の経験を生かすことができるだろうかと。良き市民となるための重要な資質とは、新しい文化において一見風変りだと思われることも理解する<u>広い心を持つこと</u>、自分の社会と他の社会における良い点と悪い点を<u>批判的な心</u>をもって<u>比較考察する</u>こと、そして自分の周りの様々な人々を温かい心をもって受け入れることだと私は気づきました。私はこれらの資質が令和を真の意味で「すべての人々のための時代」にするために役立ってくれるだろうと思います。

10-6　Japanese Speaker 3

The Heisei era was a time in which <u>rapidly</u> advancing technology changed our lives. As we enter Reiwa, the question "what are human beings?" will be asked more often than in the past. It's an era in which the strength of human connection is <u>getting weaker</u> and weaker, which is why we should <u>come out of our shells</u> and have the courage to <u>seek encounters</u> with others. Also, Japan has a role in rediscovering the natural beauty of Japanese culture and disseminating it to the world to sustain peace on this planet. The name of the new era, Reiwa, seems as if it were telling us that very thing.

10-7　Moderator 2

皆さんへ最後の問いかけです。令和への願いを叶えるために、学生として、教師として、グローバル市民として、私たち一人ひとりは何ができるでしょうか。

Culture

平成が生んだポップカルチャー

Keywords

post-WWII	名古屋外国語大学
find recognition	日本独自の
'monster movies'	『名探偵コナン』（原作：青山剛昌）
nuclear war	『ワンピース』（原作：尾田栄一郎）
Akira Kurosawa (1910-1998)	絶大
VHS video	海賊
subtitles	少年ルフィー
technically	「ひとつなぎの大秘宝」
video streaming	海洋冒険
boost (v.)	1億200万
Ghibli	人格形成
"Your Name" (Makoto Shinkai, 2016)	韓国ブーム
mainstream	『冬のソナタ』
vehicle	（KBS、2002年、ユン・ソクホ監督）
	「ヨン様ブーム」
	社会現象
	韓国大衆文化
	金大中大統領（1924-2009）
	日本大衆文化開放（1998年）
	日韓ワールドカップ共同開催（2002年）

English Speaker 1

Pop culture is an amazingly broad category. It includes not only media like TV shows, films, video games, comics, magazines and so on, but also activities such as sport, fashion, music, and dance. Of course, social media like Twitter and Instagram are included too. Since the post-WWII period Japanese pop culture found recognition in the U.S.A. and U.K.; in particular, 'monster movies' that dealt with fears over nuclear war like Godzilla, and highly skilled directors like Akira Kurosawa. It was in the 1990s, however, that Japanese pop culture exploded around the world.

通 訳

-1

English Speaker 2

The spread of Japanese pop culture, especially anime and manga, was successful partly because of its fans. Before the Heisei era it was difficult for people overseas to access anime; but in the early 1990s the increasing popularity of VHS video technology allowed fans to make copies and add foreign-language subtitles, then share the videos by mail or at university 'anime clubs'. Although this was technically illegal, it made commercial companies understand that young people abroad enjoy Japanese pop culture; this encouraged them to officially sell anime and manga.

通 訳

-2

Japanese Speaker 1

ここ名古屋外国語大学に在学している海外留学生の多くも、来日を希望した理由の一つに、日本独自のポップカルチャーの魅力を挙げています。特に、アニメ作品『名探偵コナン』、そして漫画『ワンピース』の人気は未だ絶大です。主人公の海賊となった少年ルフィーが仲間との絆に助けられ、「ひとつなぎの大秘宝」を巡って闘い続ける海洋冒険の物語です。

通 訳

●-3 | **Japanese Speaker 2**

平成はビデオゲーム文化が誕生した時代でもありました。平成元年の1989年4月、任天堂が「ゲームボーイ」を発売し、1994年には「プレイステーション」がソニーによって開発され、初代モデルは全世界で1億200万台が売り上げられる大ヒットとなりました。社会にビデオゲームが広く普及したことは、さまざまな意味で平成を生きる人々の人格形成に影響を与えました。

(通 訳)

●-4 | **English Speaker 3**

Video technology had a major influence on the spread of Japanese pop culture in developed countries. Then, in the 2000s, the Internet was popularized, and with it came many new opportunities for learning about different cultures. Online video streaming and image technologies have given a huge boost to the popularity of anime and manga; these days people from all over the world can access and enjoy it easily, and discuss it with fans from other countries on social media. Some anime like Ghibli movies and "Your Name" have actually become mainstream!

(通 訳)

●-5 | **Japanese Speaker 3**

平成は、韓流ブームに火がついた時代でもありました。2003年に韓国ドラマの『冬のソナタ』が日本で初めて放送され、「ヨン様ブーム」が社会現象となりました。このように、日本で韓国大衆文化が受け入れられた背景として、1998年に金大中大統領が表明した「日本大衆文化開放」と、2002年の日韓ワールドカップ共同開催が挙げられます。このスポーツの祭典は、今でも日韓の交友関係の再開を記念する重要な出来事として、日本、韓国の人々の記憶に刻まれています。

(通 訳)

■ Simultaneous demonstration
Culture
平成が生んだポップカルチャー

post-WWII	第二次世界大戦後
find recognition	知られるようになった
'monster movies'	「怪獣映画」
nuclear war	核戦争
Akira Kurosawa (1910-1998)	黒澤明
VHS video	ビデオテープ
subtitles	字幕
technically	本来であれば
video streaming	動画配信
boost (v.)	加速させる
Ghibli	ジブリ
"Your Name" (Makoto Shinkai, 2016)	『君の名は』
mainstream	主流
vehicle	手段

名古屋外国語大学	NUFS (Nagoya University of Foreign Studies)
日本独自の	Japan's distinctive
『名探偵コナン』（原作：青山剛昌）	"Detective Conan"
『ワンピース』（原作：尾田栄一郎）	"ONE PIECE"
絶大	massive
海賊	pirate
少年ルフィー	a boy named Luffy
「ひとつなぎの大秘宝」	'the one great secret treasure'
海洋冒険	seafaring battle adventure
1億200万	102 million
人格形成	formation of people's personalities
韓国ブーム	boom in Korean culture
『冬のソナタ』（KBS、2002年、 ユン・ソクホ監督）	"Winter Sonata"
「ヨン様ブーム」	'Bae Yong Joon boom'
社会現象	social phenomenon
韓国大衆文化	Korean culture
金大中大統領（1924-2009）	Korean President Kim Daejung
日本大衆文化開放（1998年）	open-door policy towards Japanese culture
日韓ワールドカップ共同開催（2002年）	the 2002 FIFA World Cup hosted by South Korea and Japan

●-0　English Speaker 1

ポップカルチャーとは驚くほど広いカテゴリーであり、テレビ番組、映画、テレビゲーム、漫画、雑誌などのみでなく、スポーツやファッション、音楽、ダンスなどの活動も含まれます。もちろん、Twitter や Instagram のようなソーシャルメディアさえも含まれるのです！第二次世界大戦後の時代から、日本のポップカルチャーはアメリカやイギリスで知られるようになりました。特にゴジラのような核戦争の恐怖を取り扱った「怪獣映画」や黒澤明のような才能あふれる映画監督が注目されました。日本のポップカルチャーが世界的に爆発的な人気を得たのは1990年代のことでした。

●-1　English Speaker 2

日本のポップカルチャーのなかでも、特にアニメや漫画は、ファンがいたこともあり、広まりました。平成以前では、海外の人々がアニメを見ることは難しかったのですが、1990年代初頭にはビデオテープの技術が広まったことで、ファンたちはビデオの複製ができ、外国語の字幕を付けられるようになりました。そして、郵便や大学の「アニメサークル」で、ビデオテープを共有していました。本来であれば、これは不法行為でしたが、広告会社は世界の若者たちが日本のポップカルチャーを楽しんでいるとわかり、正式にアニメと漫画を販売するに至ったのです。

●-2　Japanese Speaker 1

Many of the exchange students studying at NUFS here offer the attraction of Japan's distinctive popular culture as one of the reasons why they wanted to come to Japan. Especially, the popularity of the anime "Detective Conan" and the manga "ONE PIECE" is still massive. Talking about the manga, it is the seafaring battle adventure story of a boy named Luffy who becomes a pirate and is supported by his friends through the bonds among them, in order to win 'the one great secret treasure'.

●-3　Japanese Speaker 2

The Heisei era was also the time of the birth of video game culture. In April 1989, the first year of the era, Nintendo announced the release of the 'Game Boy,' and the 'PlayStation' was developed by SONY in 1994. The first PlayStation model became a big hit with the sale of 102 million consoles all around the world. The way the spread of video games affected society widely influenced the formation of people's personalities during the time of the Heisei era in various contexts.

●-4　English Speaker 3

ビデオの技術は、先進国における日本のポップカルチャーの広まりに大きな影響を与えました。そして、2000年代にはインターネットが普及し、それと共に異文化について学ぶ新たな機会が増えました。オンラインでの動画配信や画像処理の技術はアニメと漫画の人気を加速させました。今では世界中の人々が簡単に見ることができ、ソーシャルメディアでファン同士が語り合うこともできます。ジブリ映画や『君の名は』のようなアニメは、その主流となりました。

●-5　Japanese Speaker 3

The Heisei era can be represented as the time of a boom in Korean culture. A Korean TV show, "Winter Sonata", was broadcast in 2003 for the first time in Japan, and the 'Bae Yong Joon boom' became a social phenomenon. Following that, some factors for the acceptance of Korean culture, such as the open-door policy towards Japanese culture declared by then Korean President Kim Daejung in 1998 and the 2002 FIFA World Cup hosted by South Korea and Japan, can be mentioned. This sports festival is even now remembered both in Japan and South Korea as a vital event to celebrate the rekindling of the friendship between the nations.

TOPIC 3:
Lessons from the Covid-19 Pandemic

ポストコロナの世界を生きる
―パンデミックからの教訓

第14回 学生通訳コンテスト スクリプト
2020年11月28日 開催

話し手に語らせる

鶴田　知佳子
（学生通訳コンテスト審査員）

　通訳者として仕事をしていて常々嬉しく思うのは、難しい仕事に直面し乗り越えたあと、通訳者としてまた一回り成長した、と感じることだ。学生通訳コンテストに出場する学生の皆さんにとってもこれは同じだ。困難を感じる試練があってこそ、その向こうに成長がある。

　通訳者にとり毎回の仕事は、常に新しい。たとえ同じスピーカーの通訳であったとしても、聴衆が違えば雰囲気は変わる。前回と内容が同じでも、日によってニュアンス、口調は違う。その場におけるコミュニケーションを円滑に成り立たせるために、こちらもその場その時に合わせた口調と訳で対応する。それは苦労だが、大変楽しい苦労でもある。

　先日、我が意を得たり、と思えるような新聞記事を見つけた。翻訳家の松岡和子氏が自身の訳したシェークスピアの戯曲のなかで、「ジュリアス・シーザー」がいちばん難しかったと回想されていた記事だ（2022年5月4日朝日新聞、「人生の贈りもの　男世界の言葉　四字熟語で強く」）。

　松岡氏は男同士の気持ちの交流を描いたこの戯曲で、どう語らせようか考え悩んだ。自分は女性なので男性の気持ちを理解するのは難しいと悩んだ末、強い言葉を使おう、と思いついた。すると自分でも知らないうちに「四字熟語」を使っていたという。そのことに気付かされたのが、シェークスピアの邦訳研究で知られるダニエル・ガリモア関西学院大学教授が、南米で開かれたシェークスピア翻訳の学会で、「ジュリアス・シーザー」の松岡訳について、四字熟語の使い方を評価していたことを知った時だったという。松岡氏は、「確かに大和ことばよりは漢語の方が強い、清音よりは濁音の方が強い。あるいはアイウエオでいえばイ音やウ音より、ア音、オ音の方が強い。こう意識してはいたが、無意識のうちに選んでいた。それを聞いたときはシェークスピアになったと思いました。」と回想する。

　翻訳家・松岡氏にも、作品翻訳の苦労の中から発見があり、自身が訳している作家の声を確かに伝えられたという手応えがあった。通訳者である私にとっても、通訳した言葉はひとつの「作品」である。しかも聴き手に聞いてもらうチャンスは一回だ。その刹那の中で、聞いてわかる言葉で語り、その場にふさわしい口調で語る。聴き手に納得してもらい、会議や TV のニュース番組がスムーズに進んでいく時の喜びに勝るものはない。

鶴田　知佳子 / Tsuruta, Chikako

東京女子大学教授。東京外国語大学名誉教授。会議通訳者、放送通訳者。小学校高学年をアメリカ、高校をインドのアメリカンスクールで過ごす。上智大学外国語学部フランス語学科卒。東京銀行調査部勤務を経て、コロンビア大学経営学大学院で MBA（経営学修士）を取得。NHK 衛星放送や CNN の同時通訳者、会議通訳者などを務める。

1

Terminology and its history
用語の整理・パンデミックの歴史

Keywords

「新型コロナウイルス感染症（COVID-19）」	plague of Justinian
3・11	Black Death
象徴的な日付	vaccine
WHO（World Health Organization）	smallpox
戸惑う	a fact of life
楽観視する	depict
緊急事態宣言	inspired
行き先の見えない	allegory
閉塞感	Danse Macabre
漂う	grave (n.)
人類の歴史	vulnerable
感染症	emerge
語源	scientific knowledge
大規模に流行する	doomed to repeat
制御不能となった状態	outbreak
コロナウイルス	
ロベルト・コッホ（1843-1910）	
細菌学者	
炭疽菌	
炭疽病	
正体	
細菌の	
証明する	
結核菌	
コレラ菌	
ルイ・パスツール（1822-1895）	
予防ワクチン	
開発に成功する	

1 -0　Moderator 1

Today everyone knows the word 'pandemic'. But what exactly does it mean, and how important has it been in the history of humanity?

通　訳

1 -1　Japanese Speaker 1

「新型コロナウイルス感染症」は、3・11という象徴的な日付とともに、WHO によって「パンデミック」と宣言されました。最初は戸惑いながらも楽観視していた日本でしたが、4月7日になると政府によって緊急事態宣言が出されました。今現在も行き先の見えない閉塞感が社会全体に漂っています。ですが、歴史をよく振り返ってみると、人類の歴史は、感染症との戦いの繰り返しでもあったのです。

通　訳

1 -2　Japanese Speaker 2

「パンデミック」とは、ギリシャ語で「すべて」を意味する "pan" と、「人々」を意味する "demos" を語源とします。ある病気が世界中で大規模に流行し、制御不能となった状態を意味する用語です。WHO は従来、インフルエンザに対してのみ、この用語を使用してきましたが、WHO が「コロナウイルス」を「パンデミック」と表現するのは今回が初めてのことでした。

通　訳

1 -3　English Speaker 1

In human history, more people have died from infectious disease than anything else. In the 6th century the 'plague of Justinian' killed about half the world's population: up to 50 million people. The 'Black Death' in the 14th century killed approximately 200 million. The world's first effective vaccine – for smallpox – became available by 1796; but this disease still killed as many as 300 million people in the 20th century alone. Pandemics are a fact of human life.

通　訳

1-4　English Speaker 2

Naturally, such a major part of human history has often been depicted in art and literature. The Black Death in the 14th century inspired a famous Western allegory, the 'Danse Macabre', which means 'Dance of Death'. Many European artists drew pictures on this theme, in which a skeleton, representing Death, leads humans of all social ranks towards a grave. This art expressed that pandemics make everyone equal: it doesn't matter if you are rich or poor, you are vulnerable.

通　訳

1-5　Japanese Speaker 3

ドイツのロベルト・コッホは細菌学者であり、偉大な医師でした。1876年、コッホは炭疽菌を発見し、炭疽病の正体を明らかにします。これにより、病気は細菌に感染することによって引き起こされていると証明されたのです。この頃はまだウイルスの存在は確認されていませんでしたが、コッホはその後も結核菌やコレラ菌を発見します。そして1881年、フランスの細菌学者ルイ・パスツールが炭疽病の予防ワクチンの開発に成功すると、これを境に医学は大きく発展していくことになります。

通　訳

1-6　English Speaker 3

The COVID-19 pandemic shows the tendency of history to repeat itself. Scientists have been warning us for decades that a new infectious disease could emerge at any time and spread widely around the world. Today we travel more than ever before, which may be why this pandemic has spread so quickly. But we also have access to greater scientific knowledge than in the past. What's important is that we make good use of this knowledge while learning from history, so that we are not doomed to repeat it.

通　訳

1-7　Moderator 2

It seems that humans have always had to deal with pandemics. Now let's learn about the outbreak of COVID-19.

通　訳

① Terminology and its history
用語の整理・パンデミックの歴史

「新型コロナウイルス感染症（COVID-19）」	'novel coronavirus SARS-CoV-2' (COVID-19)
3・11	March 11
象徴的な日付	symbolic date
WHO（World Health Organization）	世界保健機構
戸惑う	be perplexed
楽観視する	be optimistic
緊急事態宣言	state of emergency
行き先の見えない	not being able to see what lies ahead
閉塞感	feeling cooped up
漂う	living with uncertainty
人類の歴史	history of humankind
感染症	infectious disease
語源	etymology
大規模に流行する	spread in a large-scale way
制御不能となった状態	uncontrollable state
コロナウイルス	coronavirus
ロベルト・コッホ（1843-1910）	Heinrich Hermann Robert Koch
細菌学者	microbiologist
炭疽菌	anthrax bacterium
炭疽病	anthrax
正体	true origin and nature
細菌の	bacterial
証明する	demonstrate
結核菌	tuberculosis
コレラ菌	cholera bacteria
ルイ・パスツール（1822-1895）	Louis Pasteur
予防ワクチン	preventative vaccine
開発に成功する	succeed in developing
plague of Justinian	ユスティニアヌスの疫病
Black Death	黒死病
vaccine	ワクチン
smallpox	天然痘
a fact of life	人間の生活
depict	描く
inspired	生み出す
allegory	寓話
Danse Macabre	死の舞踏
grave (n.)	墓場
vulnerable	危険にさらされる
emerge	発生する
scientific knowledge	科学的な知識
doomed to repeat	悲劇を繰り返す
outbreak	発生

1-0 Moderator 1

今日、誰もがパンデミックという言葉を知っています。しかし、パンデミックとは正確には何を意味し、人類の歴史においてどれほど重要な意味をもってきたのでしょうか。

1-1 Japanese Speaker 1

The 'novel coronavirus SARS-CoV-2' was declared a 'pandemic' by the WHO on the symbolic date of March 11, 2020. At first Japan was perplexed but optimistic; however, on April 7 the government declared a state of emergency. Society at large is still living with the uncertainty of feeling cooped up and not being able to see what lies ahead. Nevertheless, if we look back carefully on our history, we can see that the history of humankind has been a cycle of battles with infectious disease.

1-2 Japanese Speaker 2

The etymology of 'pandemic' is from the Greek word *pan*, meaning 'all', and *demos*, meaning 'people'. It is a term referring to a disease that spreads in a large-scale way and becomes prevalent around the world in an uncontrollable state. Until now the WHO had only used this term for influenza; this is the first time it has labelled a 'coronavirus' a 'pandemic'.

1-3 English Speaker 1

人類の歴史上、感染症で命を落とした人の数は何よりも多いのです。6世紀におけるユスティニアヌスの疫病では世界人口のおよそ半分にあたる5千万もの人が死亡しました。14世紀の黒死病では、およそ2億人が亡くなりました。1796年には既に世界初の有効な天然痘ワクチンが開発されましたが、それでも20世紀だけで3億もの人が天然痘の犠牲になったのです。このように、パンデミックは人間の生活には付きものなのです。

1-4 English Speaker 2

当然のことながら、このような人類の歴史の大部分は、しばしば芸術や文学の中に描かれてきました。14世紀の黒死病は、西洋の有名な寓話「死の舞踏」を意味する「Danse Macabre」を生み出しました。ヨーロッパの芸術家の多くは、このテーマで絵を描きました。そこでは、死を象徴する骸骨があらゆる社会階級の人間を墓場へと導く姿が描かれました。これらの絵は、パンデミックはすべての人を平等に扱う、裕福でも貧しくても誰もが危険にさらされることに変わりはない、ということを表現したのです。

1-5　Japanese Speaker 3

Robert Koch, from Germany, was a microbiologist and an outstanding physician. In 1876 Koch discovered the anthrax bacterium, clarifying the true origin and nature of anthrax. Through this he demonstrated that disease is caused by bacterial infection. At the time the existence of viruses had not been verified, but Koch later went on to discover the tuberculosis and cholera bacteria. Then, in 1881, French microbiologist Louis Pasteur succeeded in developing a preventative vaccine for anthrax, which proved a watershed moment for large developments in the study of medicine.

1-6　English Speaker 3

新型コロナウイルス感染症のパンデミックは、歴史は繰り返すという傾向を示しています。科学者たちは何十年も前から、いつ新たな感染症が発生し、世界中に広まるか分からないと警告してきました。現在、私たちはかつてないほど多くの場所を移動しており、それが今回のパンデミックが急速に広まった理由なのかもしれません。しかし、昔に比べ、科学的な知識も豊富になりました。重要なのは、歴史から学びつつ、これらの知識をうまく利用し、同じ悲劇を繰り返さないようにすることです。

1-7　Moderator 2

人類は常にパンデミックに向き合ってこなければならなかったようで。では、新型コロナウイルス感染症の発生について見ていきましょう。

2

How did it happen?

Covid-19の始まり

Keywords

detect	感染者
Wuhan	クルーズ船「ダイヤモンド・プリンセス号」
fish and live animal market	乗員
misinformation	横浜湾
contagious	隔離する
prime minister Boris Johnson (1964-)	鮮明に思い出す
admit (to hospital)	出航日
intensive care	下船する
recover	陽性と診断される
incentive	初期段階
	厚生労働省
	飛沫感染
	国民
	注意を呼び掛ける
	「エアロゾル」
	空気感染
	抑制策
	「三密」回避の徹底
	「密閉空間」
	「密集場所」
	「密接場面」
	集団感染
	リスクが高まる
	発令する
	措置をとる
	外出の制限
	商業活動の停止
	相次ぐ
	事態
	比喩
	発信する
	見受けられる

2-0 Moderator 1

COVID-19 is the first pandemic most of us have experienced, but there's a lot of confusion about its exact origins. Let's take a look at the basics.

> 通 訳

2-1 English Speaker 1

COVID-19 is one variation of a group of viruses known collectively as 'coronavirus'. It was first <u>detected</u> in the city of <u>Wuhan</u>, China, which has a large <u>fish and live animal market</u>. The virus is generally thought to have first spread through a natural process of transfer from animals to humans. Scientists have suggested two likely scenarios of how this happened, but they say it's difficult to be certain. Perhaps because of this, along with the growth of COVID-19 we have seen the growth of <u>misinformation</u> about the disease – we'll talk more about that later.

> 通 訳

2-2 English Speaker 2

The virus is highly <u>contagious</u>, so it quickly spread to other countries. The U.K. had its first cases by the end of January 2020. By the end of March the effects had become severe: some patients had died and businesses like restaurants, cinemas, bars and gyms were ordered to close. National exams for school students, which happen in July, were also cancelled. The U.K. <u>prime minister, Boris Johnson</u>, was <u>admitted</u> to <u>intensive care</u> with the virus, but luckily <u>recovered</u>. However, by the middle of August COVID-19 had caused over 45,000 deaths in the U.K.

> 通 訳

2-3 Japanese Speaker 1

日本では、乗客から感染者が出た<u>クルーズ船</u>「ダイヤモンド・プリンセス号」が2月3日に横浜に到着します。その後、<u>乗員</u>乗客合わせて約3,700人が、約ひと月にわたって<u>横浜湾</u>での<u>隔離</u>を強いられた出来事は、今でも<u>鮮明</u>に思い出されます。<u>出航日</u>の1月20日時点で感染者は一人でしたが、3月1日に全員が<u>下船</u>を果たすまでに実に705人の乗客が<u>陽性</u>と診断され、うち5名が亡くなりました。

> 通 訳

2-4　Japanese Speaker 2

初期段階で日本の厚生労働省は、ホームページで「コロナウイルスは飛沫感染によりうつる」と国民に注意を呼びかけました。その後「エアロゾル」と呼ばれる空気感染の可能性も指摘され、感染拡大の抑制策として「三密」回避の徹底が発表されました。それは、「密閉空間」、「密集場所」、「密接場面」、これらの三要素が重なったときに集団感染のリスクが最も高まるというものです。

通　訳

2-5　English Speaker 3

Different countries have taken different measures against the spread of COVID-19. For example, the U.K. was praised for some measures, such as paying up to 80% of the wages of people who lost income due to the virus. It was criticized for other things, for example a lack of clear guidance for the public on what they should and should not do. This should be a good incentive for us to think critically about how we deal with crises globally.

通　訳

2-6　Japanese Speaker 3

感染拡大に伴い、3月半ばにはイタリア、スペイン、そしてアメリカが緊急事態宣言を発令し、フランスやドイツも同様の措置を取りました。その結果、世界各国では外出が制限され、商業活動も停止されていき、各種イベントの中止も相次ぎました。このような事態を受け、各国のリーダーたちはコロナ禍の現状を「戦争」という比喩を用いて、国民にメッセージを発信することも見受けられました。

通　訳

2-7　Moderator 2

The early stages of this pandemic have shown which countries' governments and medical services were well prepared to handle a crisis, and which need improvement.

通　訳

❷ How did it happen?
Covid-19の始まり

detect	検出する
Wuhan	武漢
fish and live animal market	海鮮市場
misinformation	誤った情報
contagious	感染力がある
prime minister Boris Johnson (1964-)	ボリス・ジョンソン首相
admit (to hospital)	入院する
intensive care	集中治療室
recover	回復する
incentive	動機づけ

感染者	infected people
クルーズ船「ダイヤモンド・プリンセス号」	cruise ship 'Diamond Princess'
乗員	crew (n.)
横浜湾	Yokohama Bay
隔離する	isolate
鮮明に思い出す	clearly recall
出航日	date of setting sail, on the day the ship puts to sea

下船する	disembark
陽性と診断される	test positive
初期段階	initial stage
厚生労働省	Ministry of Health, Labor and Welfare
飛沫感染	droplet infection
国民	citizen
注意を呼び掛ける	issue an alert
「エアロゾル」	'aerosol'
空気感染	airborne infection
抑制策	measure to control
「三密」回避の徹底	carrying out a policy of 'three Cs' to be avoided
「密閉空間」	'closed spaces'
「密集場所」	'crowded places'
「密接場面」	'close-contact settings'
集団感染	mass infection
リスクが高まる	risk will rise
発令する	officially declare
措置をとる	introduce measures
外出の制限	restricted entry and exit
商業活動の停止	suspension of business activities
相次ぐ	followed by
事態	circumstance
比喩	metaphor
発信する	send
見受けられる	be obvious

2-0　　　**Moderator 1**

新型コロナウイルス感染症は、私たちの多くが初めて経験するパンデミックですが、その正確な起源については情報が混乱しています。ここでは基本的なことを見ていきましょう。

2-1　　　**English Speaker 1**

新型コロナウイルス感染症は、コロナウイルス科に属するひとつのウイルスです。最初に検出されたのは、中国の武漢市にある大きな海鮮市場でした。ウイルスは、通常まず動物からヒトに自然に感染し、拡散していくウイルスれています。科学者たちは、今回どのようにそれが起きたのか二つのシナリオを提案していますが、それを特定するのは困難です。おそらくそのためか、新型コロナウイルス感染症の増加とともに、誤った情報も広がってきています。これについては、後ほど詳しくご紹介します。

2-2　　　**English Speaker 2**

このウイルスは感染力が非常に強いので、すぐに他国へと広がりました。イギリスでは、2020年1月末に初めての感染者が出ました。3月末には患者のなかで死亡する人も出始め、レストラン、映画館、バー、スポーツジムなどのビジネスは営業停止を命ぜられるなど、影響は深刻なものとなりました。7月に行われる学生の国家試験も中止となりました。イギリスのボリス・ジョンソン首相も、新型コロナウイルス感染症に感染し集中治療室に入りましたが、幸いにも回復しました。しかしながら、イギリスでは8月中旬までに、新型コロナウイルス感染症による死者は4万5千人を超えました。

2-3　　　**Japanese Speaker 1**

In Japan, the cruise ship 'Diamond Princess' docked at Yokohama on February 3 with infected people among its passengers. Even now we can clearly recall what happened next, with approximately 3,700 crew and passengers compelled to isolate for about a month in Yokohama Bay. On the day the ship had put to sea, January 20, it had only one infected person, but by the time everyone managed to disembark on March 1, 705 passengers had tested positive; of those, five people died.

2-4　　　**Japanese Speaker 2**

In the initial stages Japan's Ministry of Health, Labor and Welfare issued an alert to citizens on its homepage, stating that "the coronavirus spreads through droplet infection." After that the possibility of airborne infection known as 'aerosol' was also identified; as a measure to control the spread of infection, it was announced that a policy of 'three Cs' to be avoided would be carried out. Those were 'closed spaces', 'crowded places', and 'close-contact settings'; when these three factors occur together the mass infection risk is most likely to rise.

2-5　English Speaker 3

新型コロナウイルス感染症の感染拡大に対しては、国ごとに異なる対策が取られています。例えば、イギリスでは、ウイルスで収入を失った人の最大80%の賃金が支払われるといった幾つかの対策が評価されました。逆に、それ以外の点では、例えば、何をすべきか、何をすべきでないのか、国民に対する明確なガイドラインの欠如が批判されました。これを機に、私たちは世界的な危機に陥ったときの対処法を批判的に考えるようになるに違いありません。

2-6　Japanese Speaker 3

Due to the spread of infection, in the middle of March Italy, Spain, and then the USA officially declared a state of emergency; countries like France and Germany also introduced similar measures. As a result, countries all over the world restricted entry and exit, followed by the suspension of business activities and cancellation of all kinds of events. Under these unfortunate circumstances leaders of various countries used the metaphor of a 'war' to refer to the coronavirus crisis, and it was obvious that they were sending a message to their citizens.

2-7　Moderator 2

このパンデミックの初期段階においては、政府や医療機関の危機管理体制が整っている国と改善が必要な国とが明らかになりました。

3

"Stay Home": A new mode of daily life

「ステイホーム」へ変化した生活スタイル

Keywords

当たり前のように	fundamentally
特別支援学校	impose
臨時休校	fine (n.)
対面を避ける	be imprisoned
消毒	vulnerable person
徹底が求められる	become universal
自粛期間	be eased
行動範囲	asymptomatic carrier
試行錯誤する	places of worship
コンテ首相（1964-）	'new normal'
不要不急の外出	immigration rules
シチリア島アグリジェント	human interaction
タンバリン	medical response
アコーディオン	
動画が全世界に流れる	
反響を呼ぶ	
現象	
品薄になる	
人気が沸騰した韓国ドラマ	
『愛の不時着』（2019年、韓国）	
国を超える	
共感し合える	

3-0 ⬛ **Moderator 1**

COVID-19 has affected the world on a large scale: economics, industry, politics, medicine, etc. But more <u>fundamentally</u> it has changed the way we live day to day.

┌─────┐
│ 通 訳 │
└─────┘

3-1　Japanese Speaker 1

未知のウイルスの出現により、それまで<u>当たり前のように</u>存在した生活習慣が全世界で激変しました。いわゆる「ステイホーム」の登場です。日本では2月27日、全国の小中高等学校、<u>特別支援学校</u>に対して<u>臨時休校</u>の要請が出され、多くの学校で卒業式や入学式が中止となりました。そしてウイルス中で<u>対面</u>を避けること、少なくとも2メートルの距離を保つ「ソーシャルディスタンス」、<u>消毒</u>、マスク着用の徹底が<u>求め</u>られました。

（ 通　訳 ）

3-2　Japanese Speaker 2

この<u>自粛期間</u>によって、<u>生活の行動範囲</u>は制限されました。と同時に、人々は在宅で可能なコミュニケーション手段を<u>試行錯誤した</u>時期であったとも言えます。例えば、ヨーロッパで深刻な被害を受けたイタリアでは、<u>コンテ首相</u>により3月11日からイタリア全土で<u>不要不急の外出</u>が禁止されます。そんな中、3月13日、<u>シチリア島アグリジェント</u>では、バルコニーで<u>タンバリン</u>や<u>アコーディオン</u>を演奏し、歌って励まし合う人々を映す<u>動画が全世界に流れ</u>、大きな<u>反響</u>を呼びました。

（ 通　訳 ）

3-3　English Speaker 1

Compared to Japan, countries like the U.K. <u>imposed</u> strict COVID-related rules on their citizens; and if you broke the rules you could be <u>fined</u> or even <u>imprisoned</u>. For example, like Italy, England imposed a national 'lockdown': the public was ordered to stay home. Going out was only allowed for grocery shopping, exercise, medical needs, or caring for a <u>vulnerable person</u>. Travelling was only allowed if absolutely necessary, and telework <u>became</u> almost <u>universal</u>. These rules <u>have been eased</u> since then, but people's daily lives were changed dramatically.

（ 通　訳 ）

3-4 English Speaker 2

At the beginning of the coronavirus outbreak, the WHO did not think wearing masks was effective. The U.K., which does not have a 'mask culture', also did not recommend using them. However, as more research was done, it was concluded that masks can help you avoid infecting other people if you are an <u>asymptomatic carrier</u>. Therefore, in August a new law was made, stating that people must wear a face covering in shops, museums, galleries, and <u>places of worship</u>. This will probably become a '<u>new normal</u>' for British society.

通 訳

3-5 Japanese Speaker 3

「ステイホーム」が始まると、ある興味深い<u>現象</u>が報告されました。例えば、バターや小麦粉、ホットケーキミックスなどの食品がスーパーで<u>品薄になり</u>ました。この現象は世界各地で起こり、それは家で過ごす子どもたちがお菓子やパンなどを作るようになったからです。またこの時期、Netflix を通して<u>人気が沸騰した韓国ドラマ</u>がありました。『<u>愛の不時着</u>』というラブストーリーです。これは、<u>国を超えて</u>人々が<u>共感し合え</u>た一つの良い社会現象であったかもしれません。

通 訳

3-6 English Speaker 3

This pandemic has affected daily life domestically, but also internationally. Many Japanese students who were enjoying study abroad had to come home. New Japanese <u>immigration rules</u> meant that Japanese citizens could come and go from the country when necessary, but foreign people living in Japan have been unable to leave, because they would not be allowed to return. This means that many of us could not visit our families, so we needed to teach our parents and grandparents to use Zoom and Skype. Changes like this have affected <u>human interaction</u> all over the world.

通 訳

3-7 Moderator 2

Our attempts to control the spread of COVID-19 have changed our daily lives, from masks to meeting people. Now let's look more deeply at <u>medical responses</u> to the pandemic.

通 訳

❸ "Stay Home": A new mode of daily life
「ステイホーム」へ変化した生活スタイル

当たり前のように	seem natural and obvious
特別支援学校	special needs school
臨時休校	temporarily close
対面を避ける	avoid face-to-face meetings
消毒	disinfection
徹底が求められる	ask to follow a policy
自粛期間	voluntary controls
行動範囲	field of activities
試行錯誤する	trial and error
コンテ首相（1964-）	Prime Minister Giuseppe Conte
不要不急の外出	non-essential and non-urgent outings
シチリア島アグリジェント	Sicily's Agrigento
タンバリン	tambourine
アコーディオン	accordion
動画が全世界に流れる	video going viral around the world
反響を呼ぶ	evoke a great response
現象	phenomenon
品薄になる	be in short supply
人気が沸騰した韓国ドラマ	be great excitement over a popular Korean drama
『愛の不時着』（2019年、韓国）	"Crash Landing on You"
国を超える	across countries
共感し合える	share feelings of empathy

fundamentally	根本的に
impose	課す
fine (n.)	罰金
be imprisoned	投獄される
vulnerable person	弱者
become universal	一般的になる
be eased	緩和される
asymptomatic carrier	無症状感染者
places of worship	礼拝所
'new normal'	「新たな日常」
immigration rules	入管法
human interaction	人間関係
medical response	医療の対応

3-0　Moderator 1

新型コロナウイルス感染症は、経済、産業、政治、医療など大きなスケールで世の中に影響を与えました。しかし、なによりも根本的に、私たちの日々の生活を変えてしまったのです。

3-1　Japanese Speaker 1

Due to the emergence of the unknown virus, all over the world people's daily habits, which had seemed natural and obvious until then, changed dramatically with the introduction of the so-called 'stay home' policy. In Japan on February 27, all elementary, junior, and senior high schools, as well as special needs schools, were requested to temporarily close; and at most schools graduation and entrance ceremonies were cancelled. In terms of daily life people were asked to follow a policy of avoiding face-to-face meetings, maintaining a 'social distance' of at least two metres, disinfecting themselves, and wearing masks.

3-2　Japanese Speaker 2

Because of these voluntary controls, our daily field of activities was limited. It can be said that it was also simultaneously a period of trial and error for people finding potential ways to communicate from home. For example, Italy in Europe was dealt grave damage, and so Prime Minister Conte forbade non-essential and non-urgent outings. During this, on March 13 in Sicily's Agrigento, video went viral around the world of people playing tambourines and accordions on their balconies and singing to cheer each other up, evoking a great response.

3-3　English Speaker 1

日本と比べると、イギリスなど他の国では、新型コロナウイルス感染症に関し、国民に厳しいルールが課せられました。それを破ると罰金や投獄されることもありました。イタリア同様、イギリスではロックダウンの実施、つまり国民はステイホームを命ぜられました。外出が許可されるのは、食料品の買い出し、運動、医療上の必要性、弱者の介護などに限られていました。移動は絶対に必要な場合にのみ許され、テレワークがほぼ一般的になりました。その後ルールは緩和されましたが、人々の日常生活は大きく変わりました。

3-4　English Speaker 2

コロナウイルスの発生当初、WHO はマスク着用に効果があるとは考えていませんでした。マスク文化のないイギリスにおいてもマスクの着用は推奨されていませんでした。しかし、研究が進むにつれ、無症状感染者であれば、マスクを着用することで他人への感染を防ぐことができると結論づけられました。そこで8月には、新しい法律が作られ、店、博物館、美術館、展示会、礼拝所などでは顔を覆うものを着用しなければならないとされました。おそらく、これがイギリス社会の「新たな日常」になるのでしょう。

3-5　Japanese Speaker 3

When 'stay home' began, some highly interesting <u>phenomena</u> were reported. For example, food products like butter, flour, and hotcake mix <u>were in short supply</u> in supermarkets. This phenomenon occurred in various places around the world, and was caused by children who had to stay at home baking cakes and bread. During this period there <u>was</u> also <u>great excitement over a popular Korean drama</u> on Netflix: a love story called "Crash Landing on You". This may be a beneficial social phenomenon that enabled people to <u>share feelings of empathy</u> <u>across countries</u>.

3-6　English Speaker 3

このパンデミックは国内だけでなく国際的にも日常生活に影響を及ぼしました。海外留学を楽しんでいた日本人学生の多くは帰国せざるを得なくなりました。日本の新しい<u>入管法</u>では、日本国民は必要に応じて国を出入りすることができましたが、日本在住の外国人は帰国が認められないため、出国することができなくなってしまいました。つまり、家族に会いに行くことができない人が多くなり、両親や祖父母にズームやスカイプの使い方を教える必要が出てきたのです。こういった変化は、世界中における<u>人間関係</u>に影響を与えました。

3-7　Moderator 2

新型コロナウイルス感染症の感染拡大を抑えるための試みは、マスクや人との出会いなど、私たちの日常生活を変えました。では、パンデミックに対する<u>医療の対応</u>について、もう少し詳しく見てみましょう。

4

The medical field: testing, care, and vaccination

医療現場とその諸問題

Keywords

financial assistance	病床不足
swift	感染症に関する法律
public health emergency	歯止めをかける
widespread	実態
increase steeply	早期発見
PPE (personal protective equipment)	早期治療
ventilator	重症化する
contribute to	死に至る
isolation	目まぐるしい
breakthrough	PCR 検査キット
dexamethasone	大量生産の
be put into use	医療メーカー
vaccine	要請する
mutate	ドライブスルー・ウォークスルー検査
extraordinary	独創的な
trial	検査体制
immune response	迅速な
test subject	MERS（中東呼吸器症候群）
	医療崩壊
	現実化
	抑制
	医療政策
	病床
	安全保障
	論説
	掲載する
	訴え

4 -0 Moderator 1

Most countries affected by the virus have supported their citizens in terms of guidelines and <u>financial assistance</u>. But the medical field is key to overcoming COVID-19.

通 訳

4 -1 English Speaker 1

The <u>swift</u> spread of COVID-19 showed that the U.K., like many other developed countries, was not well prepared to deal with a pandemic. Even after the WHO announced a <u>public health emergency</u> in January, the U.K. government did not put any strict guidelines in place or introduce <u>widespread</u> PCR testing for the virus. This was heavily criticized by medical professionals. It was not until cases <u>increased steeply</u> and hospitals ran out of beds and <u>PPE</u> that emergency hospitals were built, and testing increased to a level of 180,000 people per day.

通 訳

4 -2 English Speaker 2

The lack of <u>ventilators</u> and clear guidelines for social distancing definitely <u>contributed to</u> the high death rate in the U.K. compared to Japan. On the other hand, the huge increase in testing and <u>isolation</u> of infected people has helped decrease the number of serious cases. Also, the U.K. has made some important <u>breakthroughs</u> in drugs effective for treating COVID-19. A study led by Oxford University found that a common steroid called <u>dexamethasone</u> reduced deaths by one-third among patients on ventilators, and it <u>was put into use</u> immediately. However, most countries are hoping not only for effective treatments but also for a <u>vaccine</u>.

通 訳

4 -3 Japanese Speaker 1

日本でも4月には東京や大阪などで深刻な<u>病床不足</u>が起きました。さらに、<u>感染症に関する法律</u>がPCR検査の実施に<u>歯止めをかけた</u>ため、感染者の<u>実態</u>を正確に把握できませんでした。そもそもPCR検査は特殊なものではなく、どの病院でも日常的に実施されるものです。しかし日本の場合、従来の法律を優先したため、感染者の<u>早期発見</u>、早期治療につながらず、<u>重症化して死に至る</u>ケースが生じました。

通 訳

4-4 Japanese Speaker 2

一方、韓国で実施されたコロナ対策は実に目まぐるしいものでした。1月20日に最初の感染者が確認されると、その1週間後にPCR検査キットの開発と大量生産を医療メーカーに要請しました。その2週間後には一日当たり10万キットを生産します。それによりドライブスルーやウォークスルー検査など独創的な検査体制が可能となったのです。韓国のこの迅速で優れた医療体制は、2015年のMERS（中東呼吸器症候群）の経験があったからだと言われています。

(通 訳)

4-5 English Speaker 3

It is not yet known if a completely effective vaccine can be developed, because COVID-19, like many other viruses, could mutate and keep changing. However, scientists in several countries are currently working on vaccines at extraordinary speeds. In July another U.K. trial – also led by Oxford University – showed that their new vaccine appears to be safe and to cause an immune response in the test subjects. The next step is larger trials to check the results, but we still don't know when any vaccine will become widely available.

(通 訳)

4-6 Japanese Speaker 3

日本の医療崩壊が現実化した背景には、医療費の抑制を続けてきた国の医療政策があります。その中心は、病院・病床の削減と医師数の抑制でした。この現状に対して、5月5日の毎日新聞に「医療に安全保障の視点を」と題する論説が掲載されました。それは政府に対して「医療を安全保障の面からもとらえてほしい」という深刻な医療体制の改革を願う国民からの訴えでもあったのです。

(通 訳)

4-7 Moderator 2

We'll continue discussing medicine in an international context in the next section, when we look at the role of the World Health Organization.

(通 訳)

4 The medical field: testing, care, and vaccination
医療現場とその諸問題

financial assistance	財政援助
swift	急速な
public health emergency	公衆衛生上の緊急事態宣言
widespread	大規模な
increase steeply	急増する
PPE (personal protective equipment)	防護服
ventilator	人工呼吸器
contribute to	原因である
isolation	隔離
breakthrough	画期的な進歩
dexamethasone	デキサメタゾン
be put into use	使用される
vaccine	ワクチン
mutate	変異する
extraordinary	驚異的な
trial	臨床試験
immune response	免疫反応
test subject	被験者

病床不足	shortage of hospital beds
感染症に関する法律	laws on infectious disease
歯止めをかける	curb (v.)
実態	real state
早期発見	detect early
早期治療	treat early
重症化する	worsen
死に至る	end in one's death
目まぐるしい	rapid
PCR 検査キット	PCR testing kit
大量生産の	mass-produced
医療メーカー	medical manufacturer
要請する	call upon
ドライブスルー・ウォークスルー検査	drive-through and walk-through testing
独創的な	original (adj.)
検査体制	testing system
迅速な	prompt
MERS（中東呼吸器症候群）	MERS (Middle East Respiratory Syndrome)
医療崩壊	collapse of medical care system
現実化	realization
抑制	controlling
医療政策	medical care policy
病床	beds
安全保障	Security Guarantees
論説	editorial
掲載する	publish
訴え	appeal (n.)

4-0　Moderator 1

このウイルスの影響を受けたほとんどの国では、ガイドラインや財政援助の面で国民を支えています。しかし新型コロナウイルス感染症を克服するには、医療分野が鍵となります。

4-1　English Speaker 1

新型コロナウイルス感染症の急速な拡大は、他の先進国諸国と同様に、イギリスがパンデミックに対して準備不足であったことを示しました。1月にWHOが公衆衛生上の緊急事態宣言を出した後も、イギリス政府は厳しいガイドラインを設けたり、大規模なPCR検査を実施したりしませんでした。このことは、医療関係者から強く批判を受けました。感染者数が急増し、病院で病床や防護服が不足するようになってから、ようやく緊急病棟が建てられ、1日18万人分の検査が実施されるようになりました。

4-2　English Speaker 2

人工呼吸器の不足やソーシャルディスタンスに対する明確なガイドラインがなかったことが、日本と比べてイギリスの死亡率の高さの原因であるのは間違いありません。一方、感染者の検査や隔離が大幅に増加したことで、重篤な症例の数は減少しました。また、イギリスでは、新型コロナウイルス感染症の治療に有効な薬剤に対し画期的な進歩を遂げました。オックスフォード大学が主導した研究では、デキサメタゾンと呼ばれる一般的なステロイドが人工呼吸器を使用している患者の死亡率を3分の1分減らすことがわかり、ただちに使用されることになりました。しかし、多くの国では効果的な治療法だけでなく、有効なワクチンも期待されています。

4-3　Japanese Speaker 1

In Japan, too, cities like Tokyo and Osaka saw severe shortages of hospital beds in April. Furthermore, the laws on infectious disease curbed the implementation of PCR testing, which meant that the real state of infected persons could not be grasped. Actually, PCR tests are not something rare or special – they are routinely implemented in any hospital. However, in Japan's case the existing laws were given priority; because of this, cases occurred in which infected people were not detected or treated early, and whose illness worsened ending in their death.

4-4　Japanese Speaker 2

Conversely, the coronavirus countermeasures implemented by South Korea were very rapid. One week after identifying the first infected person, medical manufacturers were called upon to develop mass-produced PCR testing kits. A fortnight after that 100,000 kits were being produced per day. In addition, an original testing system of drive-through and walk-through testing became possible. It's said that this prompt and excellent set-up of medical care was due to South Korea's experience with MERS (Middle East Respiratory Syndrome) in 2015.

4-5　English Speaker 3

新型コロナウイルス感染症に絶対的な効果が得られるワクチンが開発できるのかはまだわかりません。というのも、新型コロナウイルス感染症は他の多くのウイルスと同様に、<u>変異して</u>変化を続けるからです。しかし、現在、様々な国の科学者たちは<u>驚異的なスピード</u>でワクチン開発に取り組んでいます。7月には、同じくオックスフォード大学主導で行われたイギリスでの別の<u>臨床試験</u>で、新しいワクチンの安全性と<u>被験者の免疫反応</u>が確認されました。次の段階は、より大規模な臨床試験でこの結果を確認することですが、どのワクチンがいつ一般に普及するのかはまだわかっていません。

4-6　Japanese Speaker 3

The background to the <u>realization</u> of the <u>collapse of</u> Japan's <u>medical care system</u> involves the continuation of national <u>medical care policies</u> with the aim of <u>controlling</u> medical expenses. Central to this were cuts to hospitals and <u>beds</u>, and controls on the number of doctors. With regard to these conditions, on May 5 the *Mainichi Shimbun* <u>published</u> an <u>editorial</u> titled 'Viewpoints on <u>Security Guarantees</u> for Medical Care'. It contained an <u>appeal</u> from the people, who wish for reform of this severe medical care system, for the government to "grasp medical care from the aspect of security".

4-7　Moderator 2

次のセクションでは WHO の役割を見ながら、引き続き国際的な面での医療について話していきましょう。

The role of the WHO (World Health Organization)

「世界保健機関（WHO）」の役割

Keywords

国際連合	incident
保健衛生機関	politicize
本部	misinformation
ジュネーブ	evolving
拠出金	U.S. President Trump (Donald John Trump; 1946-)
ワクチン接種	imply
疾病	too lenient
緊急対応	point out
取り組む	distract
注意を促す	solidarity
肺炎	contain the virus
テドロス事務局長（1965-）	
記者会見	
新型インフルエンザ	
致命的	
高齢者施設	
接触者	
追跡	
不可欠	
警鐘を鳴らす	
脱退する	
表明する	
資金	
出資する	
疾病対策	
持続	
EU 諸国	
再検討する	
改革を要請する	
反論する	

5 -0 Moderator 1

When an international health <u>incident</u> occurs, one of the main organizations responsible for handling it is the World Health Organization.

(通 訳)

5 -1 Japanese Speaker 1

WHO は1948年に設立された<u>国際連合</u>の保健衛生機関です。<u>本部</u>を<u>ジュネーブ</u>に置き、現在194ヵ国が加盟しています。加盟国の拠出金を資金とする WHO は、各種<u>ワクチン</u>接種や<u>疾病</u>に対する緊急対応などに<u>取り組ん</u>でいます。中国が WHO に新型コロナウイルスを報告したのは2019年12月21日のことでした。それを受け WHO は1月5日、世界各国に<u>注意を促し</u>、1月8日に『ウォール・ストリート・ジャーナル』は、武漢で発生したと言われているミステリアスな<u>肺炎</u>の原因がコロナウイルスであると報じました。

(通 訳)

5 -2 Japanese Speaker 2

<u>テドロス事務局長</u>は4月13日の<u>記者会見</u>で、新型コロナウイルス感染症について、2009年の<u>新型インフルエンザ</u>によるパンデミックより10倍も<u>致命的</u>だとの認識を示しました。特に<u>高齢者施設</u>など密集した環境でより簡単に広がる可能性があることを訴え、感染を<u>止め</u>るためには早期発見、検査、すべての感染者の隔離、そしてすべての<u>接触者</u>の<u>追跡</u>が<u>不可欠</u>であると改めて<u>警鐘を鳴らし</u>ました。

(通 訳)

5 -3 English Speaker 1

Yes, the WHO has clearly stated its role in handling COVID-19, and has provided countries with constant advice and updates as research into the virus progresses. Unfortunately, like a lot of other topics connected to the coronavirus, the role of the WHO has become <u>politicized</u> by many people. This is partly due to <u>misinformation</u> and lack of critical thinking, and partly to the <u>evolving</u> advice making people confused – for example the advice about wearing masks. Because of this, some people lost their trust in the organization and are refusing to listen to its advice.

(通 訳)

English Speaker 2

Some leaders, such as U.S. President Trump, criticized the WHO for being too slow to act when the virus broke out, or implied it is too lenient on China. Others point out that politicians who attack the WHO are simply trying to distract people from their own poor handling of the pandemic. On June 22 General Tedros said: "The greatest threat we face now is not the virus itself. It's the lack of global solidarity and global leadership". In order to beat this pandemic, international cooperation and trust in science are absolutely essential.

通 訳

5-5
Japanese Speaker 3

トランプ大統領は5月下旬にWHOを脱退する意向を表明し、7月には正式な手続きを開始しました。アメリカはWHOの資金の最大拠出国です。2019年度は資金額の約15%にあたる4億ドルを出資していました。このため、アメリカの脱退は、多くの疾病対策や医療プログラムの持続を脅かすものとなるでしょう。EU諸国などがトランプ大統領に再検討を求めていますが、アメリカ側はWHOが改革の要請を拒んだため、関係を断つことにしたと反論しています。

通 訳

5-6
English Speaker 3

By summer 2020 several developed countries like the U.S.A and Japan were seeing rises in the number of COVID-19 infections. But it is developing countries in South America and Africa that are suffering the most as they struggle to contain the virus. These nations need the most support from the WHO. In order to make sure this is possible, it's essential for wealthy countries to continue displaying trust in the WHO's leadership, and not threaten to cut its funding. If an investigation of the WHO's pandemic response is necessary, it can be done at a later time – today there are more important things to focus on.

通 訳

5-7
Moderator 2

The role of the WHO is a crucial one – but it can't do its job unless all nations are working together to support it.

通 訳

⑤ The role of the WHO (World Health Organization)
「世界保健機関（WHO）」の役割

国際連合	United Nations
保健衛生機関	organization for hygiene and sanitation
本部	headquarters
ジュネーブ	Geneva
拠出金	donations
ワクチン接種	vaccination
疾病	disease
緊急対応	emergency action
取り組む	tackle
注意を促す	call attention
肺炎	pneumonia
テドロス事務局長（1965-）	Director-General Tedros Adhanom Ghebreyesus
記者会見	press conference
新型インフルエンザ	novel influenza
致命的	deadly
高齢者施設	facility for the elderly
接触者	close contacts
追跡	tracing
不可欠	indispensable
警鐘を鳴らす	warn
脱退する	withdraw
表明する	announce
資金	contribution
出資する	contribute
疾病対策	disease countermeasure
持続	continuation
EU 諸国	nations of the EU
再検討する	reconsider
改革を要請する	demands for reform
反論する	argue
incident	問題
politicize	政治的に扱う
misinformation	誤った情報
evolving	次々と変わる
U.S. President Trump (Donald John Trump; 1946-)	アメリカのトランプ大統領
imply	ほのめかす
too lenient	甘すぎる
point out	指摘する
distract	目を逸らす
solidarity	連帯感
contain the virus	ウイルスを封じ込めること

5-0　　Moderator 1

国際的に健康に関する問題が起きたとき、その対応を担当する主な機関の一つが WHO、世界保健機関です。

5-1　　Japanese Speaker 1

The WHO is a United Nations organization for hygiene and sanitation, formed in 1948. With its headquarters in Geneva, it currently has 194 member nations. The WHO is funded by donations from those nations and tackles issues such as taking emergency action concerning vaccination and disease. China reported the novel coronavirus to the WHO on December 21, 2019. Upon receiving the report the WHO called the world's attention to it on January 5; on January 8 "the Wall Street Journal" reported that the cause of the mysterious pneumonia said to originate in Wuhan, China was a coronavirus.

5-2　　Japanese Speaker 2

At a press conference on April 13, Director-General Tedros indicated the WHO's recognition of the novel coronavirus being 10 times more deadly than the 2009 novel influenza pandemic. He called attention to the possibility of the virus spreading more easily in facilities for the elderly and crowded environments; and reiterated the warning that, in order to prevent infection, early detection, testing, isolation of all infected persons, and tracing of their close contacts is indispensable.

5-3　　English Speaker 1

はい。WHO は新型コロナウイルス感染症に対する役割を明確に示しており、ウイルスの研究が進むにつれ、各国に常にアドバイスや最新情報を提供してきました。しかし残念なことに、コロナウイルスに関する他の多くの話題と同じくウイルスの役割は多くの人々によって政治的に扱われています。これは、一つには、誤った情報や批判的思考の欠如が原因であり、また、マスク着用に関するアドバイスなど次々と変わるアドバイスで人々を混乱させていることも原因の一つです。このため、WHO への信頼を失い、アドバイスに耳を傾けようとしない人もいるのです。

5-4　　English Speaker 2

アメリカのトランプ大統領など一部の指導者は、ウイルス発生時の WHO の対応が遅すぎると批判したり、中国に甘すぎるとほのめかしたりしました。また別の指導者の中には、WHO を攻撃する政治家は単に自分たちのパンデミックへの対応のまずさから人々の目を逸らそうとしているだけだと指摘する人もいます。6月22日、テドロス事務局長は次のように述べています。「我々が現在直面している最大の脅威は、ウイルスそのものではありません。グローバルな連帯感とリーダーシップの欠如です。」このパンデミックに打ち勝つには、国際協力と科学への信頼が絶対に必要となります。

5-5 Japanese Speaker 3

Near the end of May, President Trump <u>announced</u> his intention <u>to withdraw</u> from the WHO, and in July began formal procedures to do so. The USA is the nation that makes the largest <u>contributions</u> to the WHO. In fiscal year 2019 it <u>contributed</u> $400,000,000, which was 15% of the total amount of donations. Because of this, the withdrawal of the USA would likely threaten the <u>continuation</u> of many <u>disease countermeasures</u> and medical care programs. The <u>nations of the EU</u> asked President Trump to <u>reconsider</u>, but the USA <u>argued</u> that because the WHO had rejected its <u>demands for reform</u>, it had decided to sever the relationship.

5-6 English Speaker 3

2020年夏には、アメリカや日本などの先進国で新型コロナウイルス感染症の感染者数が増加しています。しかし最も苦しんでいるのは南米やアフリカの発展途上国で、<u>ウイルスの封じ込め</u>に苦労しています。これらの国々は、WHO の支援を最も必要としています。そのためには、富める国が WHO のリーダーシップに信頼を寄せ続け、資金削減の脅しをかけないようにすることが不可欠です。もし WHO のパンデミック対応について調査が必要であれば、それは後回しにして、今はもっと重要なことに焦点を当てる必要があります。

5-7 Moderator 2

WHO の役割は極めて重要なものですが、すべての国が協力して支援しない限り、その役割を果たすことはできません。

6
Economic impact of the pandemic

パンデミックがもたらした経済危機

6-0   Moderator 1

The pandemic has had a huge effect on the world in an international, national, and personal context. Next to health, the biggest effect on people's lives has been related to money.

通 訳

6-1 English Speaker 1

In terms of economics, we can probably say that every country has been affected negatively. In the U.K.'s case, the early period of the pandemic caused a sharp contraction of the national GDP by 19%. This was partly because many businesses had to close temporarily, and industries like travel and hospitality almost came to a standstill. Although the economy began to grow again from May as some businesses reopened, many people's personal finances have been severely destabilized.

(通 訳)

6-2 English Speaker 2

Luckily, businesses who had difficulty paying their employees were able to apply for a fund from the government, which would pay up to 80% of the employees' wages so they would not lose their jobs. The employees could still be paid even when they couldn't go to work; this is known as a 'furlough' scheme. However, for the many people who ran their own businesses this was much more complicated, so some small entrepreneur companies had to close. Because of this people have been more wary of spending money.

(通 訳)

6-3 Japanese Speaker 1

もともと日本の経済は賃金の低下が進んでいたため、パンデミック以前から消費が著しく低迷していました。2019年10月1日には消費税が8%から10%に上がり、現状はさらに悪化したのです。そこにパンデミックが襲いました。その後、日本政府は家計への支援を目的とした緊急な経済対策として、日本に在住する人に一律10万円の給付を決めました。その給付は国籍を問わず、すべての人が対象となりました。

(通 訳)

6-4 Japanese Speaker 2

世界銀行によると、新型コロナによるパンデミックは、過去100年で最大の経済損失をもたらした感染症であることがわかっています。それは、各国政府がロックダウンや移動制限などの強硬措置をとったことに加え、人類史上最もグローバル化が進んだ経済の在り方も影響しています。日本でも失業者が9月の時点で6万人を超えました。アメリカでは2600万人以上の失業者が発生しています。今後、失業問題は世界規模でその改善に取り組む課題となるでしょう。

(通 訳)

6-5 English Speaker 3

Many governments around the world – including capitalist, socialist, and communist nations – have come under fire from their citizens who have been victims of the economic effects of COVID-19. Their economic stimulus efforts were criticized for being too slow, too small, or not reaching the people who need financial support the most. This pandemic has been a test of our leaders' ability to respond to disaster and protect their citizens. As the world begins to recover we will see which countries can find a balance between public health and a healthy economy.

(通 訳)

6-6 Japanese Speaker 3

2020年4月25日に NHK が『パンデミックが世界を変える』という対談番組を放映しました。そこに登場したフランスの経済学者ジャック・アタリ氏の発言が今でも印象深く残っています。アタリ氏は「ポジティブ経済」という用語を紹介し、これこそが今後の人類のサバイバルの鍵であると語りました。「ポジティブ経済」とは、長期的な視野に立ち、「命の産業」と呼ぶものに重点を置く経済です。つまり、生きるために必要な食糧、医療、教育、情報などの産業です。

(通 訳)

6-7 Moderator 2

Most people would argue that health is more important than the economy. But actually it's essential to balance both so ordinary people can continue living – even if our lives have been fundamentally changed.

(通 訳)

6 Economic impact of the pandemic
パンデミックがもたらした経済危機

sharp contraction	急激な減少
GDP	国内総生産
come to a standstill	行き詰まる
personal finances	懐ぐあい
destabilized	不安定な
fund (n.)	支援金
furlough scheme	一時帰休制度
entrepreneur	企業家
wary	慎重になる
capitalist	資本主義の
socialist	社会主義の
communist	共産主義の
come under fire	の非難をあびる
economic stimulus	経済刺激策
public health	国民の健康
healthy economy	健全な経済

低迷する	be sluggish
家計	household finances
緊急経済対策	emergency economic measure
一律	one-off
給付	payment
世界銀行	World Bank
経済損失をもたらす	cause economic loss
移動制限	restrictions on movement
強硬措置をとる	strict measures put in place
人類史上	human history
失業者	unemployed people
世界規模	global-scale
『パンデミックが世界を変える』	"The Pandemic Will Change the World"
対談番組	talk show
放映する	air (v.)
経済学者	economist
ジャック・アタリ（1943-）	Jacques Attali
「ポジティブ経済」	'positive economics'
人類	human race
長期的な視野	long-term outlook
「命の産業」	'life-oriented industries'
重点を置く	place emphasis on

6-0 Moderator 1

このパンデミックは世界的にも国内においても、そして個人においても大きな影響を与えました。医療の次に人々の生活に大きな影響を与えているのが、お金に関わる問題です。

6-1 English Speaker 1

経済に関して、おそらくどの国もマイナスの影響を受けたといえるでしょう。イギリスの場合、パンデミック初期段階では国内総生産が19%急激に減少しました。理由の一つとしては、多くの事業が臨時休業しなければならなくなり、旅行業や接客業といった産業は、ほぼ行き詰まったからです。事業が再開するにつれ、5月からは経済が再び成長し始めましたが、多くの国民の懐ぐあいは厳しく不安定な状態が続いています。

6-2 English Speaker 2

幸運なことに、従業員に賃金を支払うのが困難な企業は政府からの支援金に申し込むことが可能となり、それは従業員が職を失わないよう賃金の最大80%までを政府が負担するというものでした。たとえ従業員が仕事に行けなくても賃金が支払われ、これは一時帰休制度として知られています。しかしながら、個人経営の場合はより複雑で、小会社を経営する企業家らは、会社を閉じなければなりませんでした。これにより人々はお金を使うことにより慎重になっているのです。

6-3 Japanese Speaker 1

Because Japan's economy had seen a continuing decline in wages for some time, even before the pandemic consumption had been somewhat sluggish. On October 1, 2019 consumption tax was raised from 8% to 10% and conditions became even worse. Then the pandemic struck. After that, the Japanese government decided to make a one-off payment of ¥100,000 to residents in Japan as an emergency economic measure aimed at supporting household finances. This payment was not limited to Japanese citizens but was available to everyone, regardless of nationality.

6-4 Japanese Speaker 2

According to the World Bank, it is clear that the pandemic caused by the novel coronavirus has caused the greatest economic loss from any infectious disease in the last 100 years. This was influenced by the strict measures like lockdowns and restrictions on movement put in place by various governments, in addition to our current state of the largest globalization of economics in human history. In Japan, too, the level of unemployed people exceeded 60,000 in September, while in the USA there were over 26,000,000. From here on the improvement of this global-scale unemployment problem will be a challenge we have to tackle.

6-5　English Speaker 3

<u>資本主義</u>、<u>社会主義</u>、<u>共産主義国</u>を含む多くの国々の政府が、新型コロナウイルス感染症の経済的な影響によって犠牲となっている国民からの<u>非難をあびています</u>。彼らの<u>経済刺激策</u>への取り組みは遅すぎる、規模が小さすぎる、そして経済的支援を最も必要としている人たちに届いていないと批判を受けました。このパンデミックで、各国の指導者は災害時の対応力と国民を守る力があるかどうか試されています。世界中が回復し始めると、どの国々が<u>国民の健康</u>と<u>健全な経済</u>とのバランスがとれているかが、わかってくるでしょう。

6-6　Japanese Speaker 3

On April 25 this year (2020), NHK <u>aired</u> a <u>talk show</u> called "<u>The Pandemic Will Change the World</u>." The words of French <u>economist</u> <u>Jacques Attali</u>, who appeared on that program, made a deep impression that still remains. Mr. Attali introduced the term '<u>positive economics</u>', and spoke about how this could be the key to the survival of the <u>human race</u> from now on. 'Positive economics' takes a <u>long-term outlook</u>, <u>placing emphasis on</u> what are called '<u>life-oriented industries</u>': in other words, industries that provide things essential for living such as food, medical care, education, and information.

6-7　Moderator 2

多くの人々は経済よりも健康が大切であると主張するでしょう。しかし実際、私たちの生活が根本的に変化したとしても、普通の人々が生活しつづけるためには両方のバランスが必要なのです。

"Work style reform" and job-hunting for students

「働き方改革」・就職活動への影響

Keywords

就職活動	change radically
社会活動	working from home
採用活動	*hanko* stamps
合同説明会	modernize
対面面接	prospective employers
ウェブ面談	explanation sessions
積極的な導入	members of society
「働き方改革関連法」（2019年）	
施行する	
見直す	
厚生労働省	
定義	
事情に応じた	
皮肉なことに	
一気に	
就活生	
メリット	
格段と	
抵抗を感じる	
自己アピール	
表現力を磨く	
課題	

7-0   Moderator 1

The pandemic has led to major changes in the way we work. Japan is a particularly interesting case because of its traditional work style and job-hunting system.

通 訳

7-1 　Japanese Speaker 1

このコロナ禍において、日本の学生が直面する就職活動にも大きく影響を与えたといえます。ウイルスの社会活動への影響が日本で現れたのは2月下旬で、それはちょうど企業が学生の採用活動を始めた3月1日の目前のことでした。合同説明会や対面での面接、ワークショップなど、対面のイベントが中止となり、多くの企業は急遽、オンラインセミナーやウェブ面談などを積極的に導入し始めました。

```
通　訳
```

7-2 　Japanese Speaker 2

日本では2019年4月1日に「働き方改革関連法」が施行されていたので、すでに労働環境が大きく見直されていました。厚生労働省の定義によれば、「"働き方改革"とは、働く人々が、個々の事情に応じた多様で柔軟な働き方を、自分で"選択"できるようにするための改革」とあります。皮肉なことですがこのパンデミックにより、新たな働き方が一気に出現することとなったのです。

```
通　訳
```

7-3 　English Speaker 1

Working styles in most developed countries changed radically during the pandemic. The biggest change was 'telework' becoming popular. In countries like the U.K., working from home has been quite common in recent years, so the change went smoothly. But for some Japanese companies it was more difficult; although Japan has an international reputation for technology, many companies still use fax machines and need *hanko* stamps for documents. Hopefully the pandemic will help Japanese work styles modernize in future.

```
通　訳
```

7-4 | English Speaker 2

Telework has a lot of good points, but not being able to meet prospective employers face to face made it difficult for some university students when they began job hunting. As you probably know, the job-hunting process in Japan is very long and intensive compared to countries like the U.K. Students go to 'explanation sessions' and do many interviews; but with COVID-19 the usual process had to be changed, and of course this was very stressful. Fourth-year students in 2020 had to face so many challenges as they prepared to become full members of society.

通 訳

7-5 | Japanese Speaker 3

興味深いことに、就活生の半分以上がこのオンライン就活に対して、メリットを感じていると報告されています。その意見の多くに、これまでの就活生にかかった費用が格段と削減されたとありました。その一方で、面接やグループディスカッションに関しては抵抗を感じる学生が多くいたようです。オンライン上で自己アピールをしなければならないため、普段から言葉を用いて自分を表現する力を磨く必要があります。この点は今後の大学生にとって課題となるでしょう。

通 訳

7-6 | English Speaker 3

The shift to online work and job hunting has certainly caused some problems: according to "The Japan Times", job offers for graduates in 2021 dropped by 15% compared to the previous year, and doing interviews online is tough if the company isn't used to it. It has been even harder than usual for international students to find jobs. On the other hand, job hunting online means that students can apply for jobs in any part of the country without spending time and money for travelling. This is especially good for students living in rural areas.

通 訳

7-7 | Moderator 2

We should praise the students and new employees who faced the changes caused by COVID-19. It's also important to remember the bright side: with big changes come big opportunities.

通 訳

⑦ "Work style reform" and job-hunting for students
「働き方改革」・就職活動への影響

就職活動	job-hunting activities
社会活動	social activity
採用活動	employment activities
合同説明会	group information session
対面面接	in-person interview
ウェブ面談	web interview
積極的な導入	active introduction
「働き方改革関連法」（2019年）	'work-style reform bill'
施行する	execute
見直す	re-examine
厚生労働省	Ministry of Health, Labour and Welfare
定義	definition
事情に応じた	according to circumstances
皮肉なことに	ironically
一気に	all in one go
就活生	job-hunting students
メリット	benefits
格段と	dramatically
抵抗を感じる	feel some resistance
自己アピール	promote oneself
表現力を磨く	refine one's ability to express
課題	challenge (n.)

change radically	ガラリと変わる
working from home	在宅勤務
hanko stamps	押印
modernize	時代に見合ったものになる
prospective employers	受ける会社の雇い主ら
explanation sessions	説明会
members of society	社会人

7-0　Moderator 1

パンデミックは私たちの働き方に大きな変化をもたらしました。日本では独自の働き方や就職活動のやり方があります。

7-1　Japanese Speaker 1

In this coronavirus crisis, Japanese students' encounters with job-hunting activities have also been greatly affected. The effect of the virus on social activity became apparent in Japan around the end of February – right as companies began employment activities for students from March 1. Face-to-face events like group information sessions and in-person interviews, workshops, etc., were cancelled; and many companies hurriedly began the active introduction of online seminars, web interviews, and so on.

7-2　Japanese Speaker 2

In Japan on April 1, 2019 a 'work-style reform bill' was executed, so working environments had already been extensively re-examined. According to the Ministry of Health, Labour and Welfare's definition, "'work-style reform' refers to reforms in order to make it possible for workers to make their own 'choices' regarding a style of working that would be flexible according to the variety of their individual circumstances". Ironically, this pandemic has caused new working styles to arrive all in one go.

7-3　English Speaker 1

多くの先進国において、パンデミックにより働き方はガラリと変わりました。中でも最も大きな変化としては、テレワークが普及したことです。イギリスといった国では、近年在宅勤務がかなり一般的になっていたため、スムーズにテレワークに移行することが出来ました。しかし、テレワークへの移行が思うようにいかない日本の会社もありました。日本は技術分野において国際的評価が高いにも関わらず、多くの会社が未だにファックスを使い、文書には押印が必要なのです。このパンデミックによって、今後日本人の働き方が時代に見合ったものになっていくといいですね。

7-4　English Speaker 2

テレワークには多くの良い点がありますが、大学生の中には就職活動を始める際に、受ける会社の雇い主らに直接、対面で会えないのは、辛いことになります。おそらくご存じのように、イギリスのような国々に比べ、日本の就職活動は長期間かつ集中的に行われます。学生たちは説明会に行き、多くの面接を受けますが、新型コロナウイルス感染症で例年とは就職活動の過程が変わったことで、非常にストレスを受けました。2020年の4年生は、社会人になる準備として沢山の課題に直面しなければならなかったのです。

7-5 **Japanese Speaker 3**

Interestingly, over half of job-hunting students have reported that they see the benefits of online job hunting. The majority of these opinions were that their previous expenses involved in job-hunting were dramatically reduced. On the other hand, many students felt some resistance to interviews and group discussion workshops. Because they have to promote themselves online, there is a greater need than usual to refine their ability to express themselves in words. It's likely that this point will become a challenge for university students from here on.

7-6 **English Speaker 3**

オンラインワークやオンライン就活への移行は、良いことばかりではありませんでした。ジャパンタイムズによると、2021年卒への求人は前年に比べ15%落ち、会社が慣れていない場合にはオンライン面接も難しいものでした。また、留学生らは例年に比べ、仕事を見つけるのがより一層大変でした。一方、オンライン就活では、学生は日本のどの地域にある会社にも移動に時間やお金を費やさずに応募できるのです。これは特に地方に住む学生にとっては良いことといえます。

7-7 **Moderator 2**

新型コロナウイルス感染症による変化に対応しなければならなかった学生や新入社員は頑張りましたね。しかし、物事には明るい面もあるということを覚えておくことは大切です。大きな変化があると、その分機会も増えます。

The rise of misinformation

ファクトチェックの意義

Keywords

post-truth society	メルケル首相（1954-）
Oxford Languages	テレビ演説（2020年3月18日）
inaccurate information	反響を呼ぶ
be intended	透明性
deceive	視聴者
obstacle	判断能力
conservative	信憑性のない
hoax	デマ
take precautions	拡散する
conspiracy theory	排外主義的な
biological weapon	ベーガー局長
vast variety	語源
highlights	紀元前
anonymous	アテネ
violate	スパルタ
	ペロポネソス戦争（紀元前431-404年）
	民主政
	疫病
	戦争を煽る
	外敵
	「デマゴーゴス（*demagogos*）」

8-0 **Moderator 1**

Over the last few years we've learned some new phrases: fake news, fact check, <u>post-truth society</u>. All these have become deeply connected to the COVID-19 pandemic due to one of the biggest problems we had to face: misinformation.

通 訳

8-1 English Speaker 1

The definition of 'misinformation', according to Oxford Languages, is: "false or inaccurate information". Of course, all of us have the possibility of misunderstanding information sometimes, but misinformation is a little different; the second part of the definition says it is often wrong information that "is intended to deceive". And as we discussed in an earlier topic, the WHO has warned that misinformation about COVID-19 is one of the most dangerous obstacles to overcoming the virus.

通 訳

8-2 English Speaker 2

Since the outbreak of the virus there have been many examples of how misinformation has caused damage. For example, some conservative politicians and religious leaders in countries like the USA and South Korea suggested that the virus is a hoax, or that it is 'just a cold'. There have been many news reports of people who caught the virus and died because they heard this misinformation and did not take precautions. Another example is the conspiracy theory that the virus is a biological weapon created by China.

通 訳

8-3 Japanese Speaker 1

今年の3月18日に、ドイツのメルケル首相が国民に向けて行ったテレビ演説は、日本でも大きな反響を呼びました。その冒頭で首相は、「今何よりも必要とされるのは、政治において下される決定の透明性である」と語ったのです。このパンデミックにおいて国民一人ひとりが知識を共有し協力し合うことが重要で、テレビ画面の前の視聴者に対して、「あなたも真剣に考えてください」と語りました。

通 訳

Japanese Speaker 2

つまり、公正な情報の提供とそれに基づく<u>判断能力</u>が、パンデミック下を生きる人々にとって最も必要とされるということです。ですが、全世界では<u>信憑性</u>のない情報やデマが<u>拡散</u>しており、「デマデミック」と呼ばれる新たな社会現象が起こっています。中には、<u>排外主義</u>的な情報もあり、これを受け、UNESCO のベーガー局長は各国政府に対して、透明性のあるデータを積極的に公開するよう促しました。

（ 通 訳 ）

8 -5

English Speaker 3

The <u>vast variety</u> and quick spread of misinformation in this pandemic <u>highlights</u> the importance of critical thinking skills: the ability to compare and evaluate information in order to judge what we can rely on. This has become even more crucial lately, as misinformation is not spread only by <u>anonymous</u> people on the Internet. Unfortunately, we have seen national leaders promote false information too. In fact, in August 2020 Twitter and Facebook removed a post by US President Trump for <u>violating</u> their rules about COVID-19 misinformation.

（ 通 訳 ）

8 -6

Japanese Speaker 3

「デマ」の<u>語源</u>は<u>紀元前</u>の出来事に由来します。<u>アテネ</u>が<u>スパルタ</u>とペロポネソス戦争をしていた時、アテネの<u>民主政</u>を完成させた優秀な指導者ペリクレスが<u>疫病</u>で亡くなりました。その後、別の指導者が現れ、<u>戦争を煽る</u>ようなことをしたのです。このように、<u>外敵</u>を作り国民の支持を得ようとした政治家を、ギリシャ語で「<u>デマゴーゴス (demagogos)</u>」と呼び、これが日本語の「デマ」の語源となりました。

（ 通 訳 ）

8 -7

Moderator 2

The problem of misinformation shows the need for critical thinking. In a pandemic situation perhaps we should rely on information from scientific experts instead of politicians.

（ 通 訳 ）

8 The rise of misinformation
ファクトチェックの意義

post-truth society	ポスト真実社会
Oxford Languages	オックスフォード辞典
inaccurate information	不正確な情報
be intended	意図的に
deceive	欺く
obstacle	障害
conservative	保守的な
hoax	でっち上げ
take precautions	予防する
conspiracy theory	陰謀論
biological weapon	生物兵器
vast variety	多様性
highlights	浮き彫りにする
anonymous	匿名の
violate	反する

メルケル首相（1954-）	Chancellor Angela Dorothea Merkel
テレビ演説（2020年3月18日）	address on television
反響を呼ぶ	make a splash
透明性	make transparent
視聴者	viewers
判断能力	ability to make judgements
信憑性のない	not be authenticated
デマ	misinformation (*dema*)
拡散する	spread (v.)
排外主義的な	anti-foreign exclusivism
ベーガー局長	Director Guy Berger
語源	etymology
紀元前	B.C. era
アテネ	Athens
スパルタ	Sparta
ペロポネソス戦争（紀元前431-404年）	Peloponnesian War
民主政	democracy
疫病	plague
戦争を煽る	fan the flames of war
外敵	foreign enemy
「デマゴーゴス（*demagogos*）」	*demagogos*

8-0　Moderator 1

ここ数年で、私たちはフェイクニュース、ファクトチェック、ポスト真実社会といった新しい語彙を学びました。これらの用語は新型コロナウイルス感染症と深く関わっています。それは私たちが最も真剣に受け止めなければならない誤情報という問題のためです。

8-1　English Speaker 1

オックスフォード辞典によると、「誤情報」の定義は、「誤った、あるいは不正確な情報」です。もちろん、すべての人が時に情報を誤解してしまうことがありますが、誤情報とは少し違うものです。二つ目の定義は、誤情報は「人を意図的に欺くための」間違った情報と示されています。そして前のトピックでも語ったように、WHO は新型コロナウイルス感染症に関する誤情報がウイルスを克服する上での最も危険な障害の一つとなっていると警告しています。

8-2　English Speaker 2

ウイルスの発生以来、誤情報によって発生した被害の例が多く挙げられています。例えば、アメリカや韓国の保守的な政治家や宗教指導者たちは、ウイルスはでっち上げである、あるいは単なる風邪に過ぎないと示唆しています。この誤情報を聞き予防をしていなかったためにウイルスに感染し死亡した人々のニュースが後を絶ちません。他の例として、ウイルスは中国によって作られた生物兵器であるという陰謀論もあります。

8-3　Japanese Speaker 1

On March 18 this year, Germany's Chancellor Merkel addressed the nation on television in a speech that made a big splash in Japan. The Chancellor began by saying: "What is more important than anything is that we make political decisions transparent." In this pandemic it is vital that all citizens share their knowledge and cooperate with each other; to the viewers in front of their televisions she said: "Please consider this seriously."

8-4　Japanese Speaker 2

In other words, the most important thing for people living in the shadow of the pandemic is the provision of impartial information and the ability to make judgements based on that information. However, information that has not been authenticated, as well as misinformation (dema), is spreading all over the world, and a new social phenomenon known as a demademic is occurring. This includes information with an anti-foreign exclusivism; in response to this, Director Berger at UNESCO called for all nations' governments to actively make transparent data available to the public.

8-5　English Speaker 3

このパンデミックにおける誤情報の多様性と急速な広がりは、何に頼るべきかを判断するために情報を比較し評価する能力である、批判的思考をもつ大切さを浮き彫りにしました。これらの誤情報がネット上で匿名の人によってのみ拡散されているわけではないため、これは最近になってより深刻になりました。残念なことに、国の指導者が誤った情報を促進している姿も見られました。実際、2020年8月、新型コロナウイルス感染症の誤情報に関わる規則に反しているとして、ツイッターとフェイスブックはアメリカのトランプ大統領の投稿を削除しました。

8-6　Japanese Speaker 3

The etymology of *dema* comes from an incident in the B.C. era. During the Peloponnesian War between Athens and Sparta, the great leader Pericles, who accomplished democracy in Athens, died of the plague. Following this a different leader emerged, fanning the flames of war. In this way, politicians who create a foreign enemy to secure the support of their citizens are called *demagogos* in Greek, which is the origin of the Japanese word *dema*.

8-7　Moderator 2

誤情報の問題は批判的思考の必要性を示しています。パンデミックの状況において、私たちは政治家ではなく科学の専門家による情報を信頼すべきなのかもしれません。

9

Community spirit
共同体としての相互援助

Keywords

国連事務総長
アントニオ・グテーレス（1949-）
「グローバル停戦の呼びかけ」（3月24日）
民族性
党派
宗派
容赦なく
紛争
終止符を打つ
荒廃する
『TIME』誌
世界的な反響を呼ぶ
執筆者
『サピエンス全史』（2015年）
名を馳せる
イスラエル人歴史学者
ユヴァル・ノア・ハラリ（1976-）
連帯
打ち勝つ
唯一の道
全世界共通の敵
一致する
国際協調
ノーベル平和賞
飢餓
食料援助
「国連世界食糧計画（WFP）」
シリアやイエメンの内戦
ロヒンギャ難民（ミャンマー少数民族）

good deed
initially
be ostracized
gotong royong
aspect
keep one's eyes open

9-0　Moderator 1

We've heard about the problems and challenges caused by COVID-19. But this pandemic has also shown us the good in people.

通 訳

9-1　Japanese Speaker 1

国連事務総長のアントニオ・グテーレス氏は3月の下旬、世界各国に向けて重要なメッセージを投げかけました。それは、「グローバル停戦の呼びかけ」でした。このウイルスは、国籍も民族性も、党派も宗派も関係なく、すべての人を容赦なく攻撃する。全世界では激しい紛争が続いているため、まずは「戦争という病」に終止符を打ち、私たちの世界を荒廃させているこのウイルスと闘うことが重要であると訴えました。

通 訳

9-2　Japanese Speaker 2

また3月15日付けの『TIME』誌に非常に興味深い記事が掲載され、世界的な反響を呼びました。執筆者は、『サピエンス全史』で名を馳せたイスラエル人歴史学者ユヴァル・ノア・ハラリです。ハラリ氏はそのなかで、「ハイレベルのグローバルな信頼と連帯がコロナに打ち勝つ唯一の道である」と述べています。コロナは全世界共通の敵であるため、その敵に対してバラバラに闘うのではなく、今こそ全世界が一致して国際協調を目指すべきだと訴えました。

通 訳

9-3　English Speaker 1

On a local level there have been many examples of people coming together as a community to help and encourage one another. All over the world we have seen examples of good deeds. In the U.K. volunteers got together to deliver food and medicine to vulnerable people in their local area; they used social media to communicate and get information about who needed help. Families with children also put pictures of rainbows in their windows to cheer people up as they walk past.

通 訳

9-4 English Speaker 2

In some countries, trust in the national leaders has decreased since the outbreak of the virus; this means that local leaders have had a more important role to play. In West Java, Indonesia there was <u>initially</u> worry and panic when COVID-19 spread, and the first man to be infected <u>was ostracized</u>. But after the community leaders gave calm advice the residents started to be more supportive, and now are providing food and masks to vulnerable people. In Indonesia this community spirit is known as *gotong royong*.

通 訳

9-5 Japanese Speaker 3

10月9日、今年の<u>ノーベル平和賞</u>が発表され、紛争や<u>飢餓</u>に苦しむ人々に<u>食糧援助</u>を行う<u>「国連世界食糧計画（WFP）」</u>が選ばれました。1963年に設立されたこの国際機関は近年、<u>シリアやイエメンの内戦</u>、さらに、<u>ミャンマーの少数派ロヒンギャ難民</u>への支援に取り込んでいました。またこのパンデミックを受け、学校に通えなくなった発展途上国の子どもたちに給食に代わる食糧を届ける活動も行っています。世界にはコロナに加え、より過酷な現状の下で生活を強いられている多くの人々がいること忘れてはいけません。

通 訳

9-6 English Speaker 3

It's true that since the pandemic began we have seen some of the most negative <u>aspects</u> of humanity: nationalism, discrimination, selfishness, and lack of critical thinking. But this crisis has also helped many of us be more aware of what we can do to help the people around us. There are things everyone can do to make sure we overcome the pandemic together, so we should all <u>keep our eyes open</u> and find out how we can assist our local community.

通 訳

9-7 Moderator 2

We've looked at a wide range of topics today. To wrap up, let's think a little about what life could be like after the COVID-19 pandemic.

通 訳

⑨ Community spirit
共同体としての相互援助

国連事務総長	UN Secretary General
アントニオ・グテーレス（1949-）	António Manuel de Oliveira Guterres
「グローバル停戦の呼びかけ」（3月24日）	'appeal for a global ceasefire'
民族性	race (n.)
党派	faction
宗派	denomination
容赦なく	relentlessly
紛争	conflict (n.)
終止符を打つ	put a stop to
荒廃する	devastate
『TIME』誌	"TIME" magazine
世界的な反響を呼ぶ	spark an international response
執筆者	author
『サピエンス全史』（2015年）	"Sapiens: A Brief History of Humankind"
名を馳せる	win fame
イスラエル人歴史学者	Israeli historian
ユヴァル・ノア・ハラリ（1976-）	Yuval Noah Harari
連帯	solidarity
打ち勝つ	conquer
唯一の道	sole path
全世界共通の敵	common enemy of the entire world
一致する	come together
国際協調	international cooperation
ノーベル平和賞	Nobel Peace Prizes
飢餓	famine
食料援助	food aid
「国連世界食糧計画（WFP）」	United Nations World Food Program
シリアやイエメンの内戦	civil wars in Syria and Yemen
ロヒンギャ難民	Rohingya refugees
（ミャンマー少数民族）	（a minority group from Myanmar）

good deed	善い行い
initially	最初は
be ostracized	追放される
gotong royong	「ゴトンロヨン」
aspect	側面
keep one's eyes open	周りを見渡す

⑨-0 Moderator 1

新型コロナウイルス感染症によって起きた問題や課題についてこれまで話してきましたが、このパンデミックでは人々の良い面も見ることができました。

⑨-1 Japanese Speaker 1

In the second half of March, UN Secretary General António Guterres gave an important message to all the nations of the world: an 'appeal for a global ceasefire'. This virus relentlessly attacks all people regardless of nationality or race, faction or denomination. Likewise, Mr. Guterres stressed that the continuing violent conflict worldwide means that what is important in fighting this virus, which is devastating our world, is to first put a stop to 'the disease called war'.

⑨-2 Japanese Speaker 2

Furthermore, an extremely interesting article was published in the March 15 edition of "TIME" magazine, sparking an international response. The author was Israeli historian Yuval Noah Harari, who won fame with his book "Sapiens: A Brief History of Humankind". In the article, Mr. Harari states that "a high level of trust and solidarity" on a global scale is the sole path to conquering the coronavirus. The virus is the common enemy of the entire world, he argues; so, rather than fighting that enemy in a scattered way, now is the time for the whole world to come together and aim for international cooperation.

⑨-3 English Speaker 1

地域レベルにおいて、コミュニティとして互いに助け励まし合い人々が一丸となる例が多くあります。世界中で、善い行いが見られました。イギリスではボランティアが集まり、食料や医薬品を地域の必要としている人々に届けました。ソーシャルメディアを通じて、連絡を取り合い、誰が助けを必要としているかという情報も入手したのです。子どものいる家庭では通りすがりの人々を元気づけるために窓に虹の絵を飾るということもありました。

⑨-4 English Speaker 2

新型ウイルスの発生後、国の指導者たちへの信頼を損ねてしまった国もあります。そのような国では、地域のリーダーたちは、より重要な役割を果たさなければならなかったのです。インドネシアの西ジャヴァ州では新型コロナウイルス感染症が拡大した際、最初は心配やパニックが起こり、一人目の感染者は地域から追放されてしまいました。しかし、その地域のリーダーたちが冷静なアドバイスをすると、住民たちは協力的となり、今では助けを必要とする人々に食料やマスクを提供するまでとなりました。インドネシアでのこのコミュニティスピリット、地域魂は「ゴトンロヨン」として知られています。

9-5 　Japanese Speaker 3

On October 9 the 2020 <u>Nobel Peace Prizes</u> were announced: the <u>United Nations World Food Program</u>, which gives <u>food aid</u> to people suffering from conflict and <u>famine</u>, was chosen. This international organization was founded in 1963; in recent years it has given support during <u>civil wars in Syria and Yemen</u>, and also to the <u>Rohingya refugees</u>, a minority group from Myanmar. It is also working to provide staple foods in lieu of school lunches to children in developing countries who have been unable to attend school during this pandemic. We must not forget that there are many people in the world who, in addition to the coronavirus, are forced to live their lives in even harsher conditions.

9-6 　English Speaker 3

パンデミックが始まって以来、国家主義、差別、利己心、批判的思考の欠如といった人間のもっともネガティブな<u>側面</u>の数々を目の当たりにしました。しかしこの危機は私たちの周りの人々を助けるために何ができるかも気づかせてくれました。パンデミックを共に乗り越えるために誰もが協力してできることがあります。ですから、私たちは常に<u>周りを見渡して</u>、地域コミュニティをいかに支援できるかを考えていくべきです。

9-7 　Moderator 2

今日、私たちは様々なトピックに注目してきました。まとめとして、新型コロナウイルスのパンデミック後の生活がどうなるのか少し考えてみましょう。

10

Living in a post-Corona world

ポストコロナを生きるために

Keywords

be distributed	人類
be alert	信頼の欠如
be suited to	専門家
living in isolation	公的機関
socializing	故意に
indispensable	損なう
scientific literacy	格差
formal education	浮き彫りにする
simultaneously	長期化する
embrace (v.)	世界的経済危機
rebuild	対立
unpredictable	憎悪
	資源の奪い合い
	駆り立てる
	ジョージ・フロイド（1973-2020）
	「ブラック・ライブズ・マター」
	抗議運動
	飛び火する
	豊かさ
	不幸
	特徴
	分断する
	はびこる
	共存

10-0　Moderator 1

Even after an effective vaccine for COVID-19 is found and <u>distributed</u>, the impacts of this pandemic will probably be with us for many years to come.

(通　訳)

10-1　English Speaker 1

Actually, it's not easy to predict what the world will look like after the pandemic is over. As one BBC Future article points out, similar diseases could appear at any time and so we should continue to <u>be alert</u>. On the other hand, most people <u>are</u> not <u>suited to living in isolation</u>, and so societies must adapt in order to safely reintroduce social opportunities. This requires a high level of hygiene in public spaces like restaurants and gyms so people can feel secure; for example using digital menus instead of paper ones. Perhaps eating and <u>socializing</u> outside will also become more common.

(通　訳)

10-2　English Speaker 2

One of the key areas that could change in future is education. We've already seen that logical and critical thinking is <u>indispensable</u> to keeping a society safe, and this needs to be taught from a young age. UNESCO says it is more important than ever to include <u>scientific literacy</u> in school curriculums. It also suggests creating new ways of learning that mix in-person classes with online activities. At the same time, we should develop more materials and technologies that are freely available to students around the world, including to students who don't have access to <u>formal education</u>.

(通　訳)

10-3　Japanese Speaker 1

今日、<u>人類</u>が深刻な危機に直面しているのは新型コロナウイルスのせいばかりではなく、人間同士の<u>信頼の欠如</u>の結果でもあります。感染症を打ち負かすためには、人々は科学の<u>専門家</u>を信頼し、国民は<u>公的機関</u>を信頼し、各国は互いを信頼する必要があります。この数年間、多くのリーダーたちが、科学や公的機関、また国際協力に対する信頼を、<u>故意に損なって</u>きました。その結果、グローバルな視点を持った指導者が不在の状態で、今回の危機に直面しているのです。

(通　訳)

Japanese Speaker 2

またこのパンデミックは、社会における格差や不平等を浮き彫りにしました。今後長期化が想定される世界的な経済危機は、対立や憎悪、また資源の奪い合い等へと人々を駆り立てる危険性があります。5月にアメリカのミネアポリスでジョージ・フロイドさんが警察官によって殺害された事件も、まさにこの社会に存在する不正を表す出来事でした。その後、全米で「ブラック・ライブズ・マター」による抗議運動が起こり、世界各地へ飛び火しました。

(通 訳)

English Speaker 3

As you said, it's likely that in future we'll have to live while simultaneously managing the COVID-19 problem and dealing with other social issues. Each society will need to balance keeping people safe and healthy with other human rights. We must move beyond the negative impacts and embrace the positive ones. On an individual level the changes caused by the coronavirus could give us an opportunity to improve our work-life balance. We also have a chance to rebuild our economies in a way that recognizes the important connection between human beings and the environment.

(通 訳)

Japanese Speaker 3

このパンデミックは、豊かさだけではなく、不幸も国境を越えて共有するのがグローバル化の特徴だと私たちに知らしめました。国籍や言語の違いで人々が分断される中、外国語を学ぶ意味はより重要性を持つことでしょう。世界を分断から守るには、自分と異なる他者を知らなければいけません。それぞれの言語を母語とする人や文化を尊重することを通して、この社会にはびこる差別や憎しみを克服することができます。私たちはどのような状況にあったとしても、他者との共存を忘れてはいけません。

(通 訳)

Moderator 2

The future is unpredictable when it comes to COVID-19. But we shouldn't just 'wait and see' what it will be like; we should each make an active effort to guide our world in a positive direction.

(通 訳)

10 Living in a post-Corona world
ポストコロナを生きるために

be distributed	行き渡る
be alert	警戒する
be suited to	慣れる
living in isolation	隔離生活
socializing	交流の機会
indispensable	不可欠である
scientific literacy	科学リテラシー
formal education	正式な学校教育
simultaneously	同時に
embrace (v.)	受け入れる
rebuild	再構築する
unpredictable	先行き不透明な

人類	humanity
信頼の欠如	lack of trust
専門家	expert (n.)
公的機関	public institution
故意に	deliberately
損なう	damage (v.)
格差	disparity
浮き彫りにする	throw into relief
長期化する	lengthen
世界的経済危機	worldwide economic crisis
対立	antagonism
憎悪	hatred
資源の奪い合い	scramble for resources
駆り立てる	propel
ジョージ・フロイド（1973-2020）	George Floyd
「ブラック・ライブズ・マター」	'Black Lives Matter'
抗議運動	demonstrations
飛び火する	spread (v.)
豊かさ	wealth and plenty
不幸	misfortune
特徴	feature (n.)
分断する	divide
はびこる	run rampant
共存	coexist

10-0 Moderator 1

たとえ、新型コロナウイルス感染症への効果的なワクチンが見つかり、人々に行き渡ったとしても、このパンデミックの影響はおそらくこの先何年も続くのでしょう。

10-1 English Speaker 1

実際、パンデミックが収束した後の世界を予測することは簡単ではありません。BBC Future のある記事は、似たような病気はいつ発生してもおかしくないため、私たちは警戒し続けなければならないと指摘しています。一方、多くの人々は隔離生活に慣れてはいないため、社会は人々との交流の機会を、安全を確保しつつ再導入しなければなりません。これには、人々が安心できるようレストランやジムといった公共スペースでの高い衛生レベルが必要不可欠であり、例としては、紙のメニューの代わりにデジタルメニューを使うということがあげられます。おそらく外食や外での交流の機会はより一般的になっていくでしょう。

10-2 English Speaker 2

将来変わるであろう重要な分野は教育です。これまでに論理的、批判的思考は社会を安全に保つために不可欠であると論じてきましたが、このような思考は若いうちから教育されるべきことです。UNESCO は科学リテラシーを学校のカリキュラムに入れることがこれまで以上に重要であると訴えています。さらにオンライン上でのアクティビティと対面授業を合わせた新しい学習法を作ることを提案しています。同時に、正式な学校教育を受けることのできない世界中の学生たち誰もが自由に利用できる教材やテクノロジーの開発を行っていくべきでしょう。

10-3 Japanese Speaker 1

The serious crisis facing humanity today is not only the fault of the novel coronavirus – it is also a consequence of the lack of trust between humans. In order to defeat infectious disease people must trust scientific experts; citizens must have faith in public institutions; and nations must have confidence in each other. In the past several years many leaders have deliberately damaged trust in science, public institutions, and international cooperation. As a result, we are confronting the current crisis without leaders who possess a global outlook.

10-4 Japanese Speaker 2

Furthermore, this pandemic has thrown into relief the disparities and inequality in society. There is a danger that it will propel people towards a worldwide economic crisis – which is hypothesized to lengthen from now own – antagonism and hatred, and a scramble for resources. The murder of George Floyd by a police officer in Minneapolis, USA in May 2020 seemed an incident that precisely represents the injustice present in society. Following that, demonstrations by 'Black Lives Matter' occurred in America and spread across the world.

English Speaker 3

おっしゃるように、将来私たちは新型コロナウイルスへの問題に対処すると同時に、他の社会問題についても対処していかなければならないかもしれません。それぞれの社会は、人々の安全と健康とともに他の人権についてもバランスをとっていく必要があるでしょう。マイナスの影響を乗り越えて、前向きな面を受け入れていかなければなりません。個人の生活においては、このコロナウイルスがもたらした変化はワークライフバランスを改善するよい機会となりました。さらに私たちには人間と環境との重要な関わりを考慮しながら経済を再構築するという貴重な機会でもあるのです。

10-6

Japanese Speaker 3

From this pandemic we have learned that not only wealth and plenty but also misfortune is shared beyond national borders as a feature of globalization. While we are divided by differences in nationality and language the study of foreign languages assumes even more importance. To guard our world from division we must get to know other people who differ from ourselves. By respecting the culture from which each language comes, and the people who speak it as their mother tongue, we can overcome the discrimination and hatred that run rampant in our society. We must not forget that, no matter what the circumstances, we coexist with others.

10-7

Moderator 2

新型コロナウイルス感染症に関しては、先行き不透明です。しかし私たちは単にどうなるかを待ち続けるだけでなく、一人ひとりが世界を良い方向に積極的に導いていかなければいけません。

The role of arts and literature

「芸術と文学の役目」の登場

Keywords	
memorializing	『ペスト』（1947年）
the human condition	ナチス
contagious disease	たとえる
Albert Camus (1913-1960)	人間の力
José Saramago (1922-2010)	混乱する
Ling Ma (1983-)	立ち向かう
repressive	徹底した
group-think	考察する
Virginia Woolf (1882-1941)	立ち上がる
trials (difficulties, challenges)	次世代が引き継ぐ
characterize	文芸誌
pathologize	相次いで
Fyodor Dostoevsky (1821-1881)	最新号
"Crime and Punishment" (1866)	特集を組む
Italian Renaissance	舞台
Girolamo Fracastoro (1476-1553)	医療従事者
Syphilis	宅配業者
	レジを打つ人
	追い詰められる
	トラウマ
	人間の共感力
	養う
	登場人物
	医者リウー
	新聞記者ランベール
	ヒロイズム
	誠実さ
	唯一の方法
	ポストコロナ
	私たちに大切なヒントを投げかける

●-0 English Speaker 1

The Covid-19 crisis has had a severe impact on the arts and entertainment industry, with galleries and theatres closed and performers of all kinds put at economic risk. And yet the arts have never been more important than when they are documenting and <u>memorializing</u> crisis moments in human history. We can learn a great deal about the current pandemic by looking to the art and literature of the past; and, beyond this, we can hope to more deeply understand <u>the human condition</u>.

通 訳

●-1 English Speaker 2

Illness in literature is often used not as a simple description of a disease, but as a metaphor for a contemporary social problem. For example, <u>contagious disease</u> has been used by authors like <u>Albert Camus</u> in 1947, <u>José Saramago</u> in 1995, and <u>Ling Ma</u> in 2018 to represent the dangers of quick-spreading, <u>repressive</u> 'group-think' – essentially the lack of independent, critical thinking. Other writers, like <u>Virginia Woolf</u> in 1925, focus on the shared emotional and mental <u>trials</u> of people living through a health crisis. Pandemic literature is never simply about disease.

通 訳

●-2 Japanese Speaker 1

ここ日本でも、カミュの『ペスト』がベストセラーになっています。1947年に発表されたこの作品は、その2年前に終わった戦争や<u>ナチス</u>をペストに<u>たとえ</u>、<u>人間の力</u>を超えた大きな力に社会が襲われた時、人々はどのように<u>混乱し</u>、どのように<u>立ち向かう</u>かを<u>徹底して考察する</u>小説です。作品の中でも多くの人々が亡くなりますが、そのとき患者の命を救うために<u>立ち上がった</u>人たちもいて、その記憶は決して忘れてはならず、それを<u>次世代</u>が引き継いでほしいとカミュは願ったのかもしれません。

通 訳

Japanese Speaker 2

今回のコロナ禍を受け、日本の文芸誌は相次いで最新号で特集を組み、感染が広がる社会を舞台にした小説などを掲載しています。その主題は、医療従事者から宅配業者、スーパーでレジを打つ人々、あるいは経済的に苦しい中で追い詰められていく人などです。今後は、特に辛い状況を経験した人々のトラウマを、社会がどう受け止めていくかが問われていく時代になります。その時、文学、そして芸術といった人間の共感力を養ってくれる分野が、これまで以上に重要な役目を果たすことが期待されているのです。

(通 訳)

-4

English Speaker 3

Storytelling shapes how we characterize illness. One tendency writers have during a health crisis is to pathologize the disease: to find someone to blame. Just as Covid-19 has been called 'the Chinese virus', Dostoevsky in "Crime and Punishment" called the mysterious disease that swept Russia 'the Asian fever'; while Italian Renaissance poet Girolamo Fracastoro defined syphilis as 'the French disease'. Past literature shows that humans have always had trouble coming together instead of splitting apart during crisis moments.

(通 訳)

-5

Japanese Speaker 3

小説『ペスト』の登場人物の一人である医者のリウーが、作中で若い新聞記者ランベールにこう語る場面があります。「今回の災厄では、ヒロイズムは問題じゃないんです。問題は、誠実さということです。こんな考えは笑われるかもしれないが、ペストと闘う唯一の方法は誠実さです」。それを聞くランベールは、その「誠実さ」の意味について質問します。リウーはこう返しました。「一般的にはどういうことか知りません。しかし私の場合は、自分の仕事を果たすことだと思っています」。このメッセージは、ポストコロナを生きようとする私たちに大切なヒントを投げかけてくれています。

(通 訳)

通　訳

■ Simultaneous demonstration
The role of arts and literature
「芸術と文学の役目」の登場

memorializing	記憶に残すこと
the human condition	人間の本性
contagious disease	疫病
Albert Camus (1913-1960)	アルベール・カミュ
José Saramago (1922-2010)	ジョゼ・サラマーゴ
Ling Ma (1983-)	リンマ
repressive	抑圧的な
group-think	集団思考
Virginia Woolf (1882-1941)	ヴァージニア・ウルフ
trials (difficulties, challenges)	試練
characterize	性格を形づける
pathologize	病理化する
Fyodor Dostoevsky (1821-1881)	ドストエフスキー
"Crime and Punishment" (1866)	『罪と罰』
Italian Renaissance	イタリア・ルネッサンス
Girolamo Fracastoro (1476-1553)	ジローラモ・フラカストロ
Syphilis	梅毒

『ペスト』（1947年）	"La Peste"
ナチス	Nazis
たとえる	liken
人間の力	human capabilities
混乱する	fall into chaos
立ち向かう	oppose
徹底した	thorough
考察する	consideration
立ち上がる	take action
次世代が引き継ぐ	pass on to the next generation
文芸誌	literary magazine
相次いで	one after another
最新号	latest issues
特集を組む	put together special edition
舞台	setting
医療従事者	healthcare workers
宅配業者	delivery drivers
レジを打つ人	cashiers
追い詰められる	be trapped in
トラウマ	trauma
人間の共感力	humans' empathetic powers
養う	cultivate
登場人物	characters
医者リウー	doctor named Rieux
新聞記者ランベール	newspaper reporter, Rambert
ヒロイズム	heroism
誠実さ	common decency
唯一の方法	only means
ポストコロナ	post-corona world
私たちに大切なヒントを投げかける	an important hint given to all of us

-0　English Speaker 1

新型コロナウイルス感染症という危機は、芸術や芸能分野にも厳しい影響を与え、美術館や劇場は閉鎖となり、芸術家らは経済的な危機に直面しています。しかし一方で、人類の歴史における危機を文字化し、記憶に残すことほど芸術の役割として重要なことはありません。私たちは現在の危機について、過去の芸術や文学作品を見ることで、様々なことを知ることができます。そして、さらに人間の本性についてより深く知ることができるのではないでしょうか。

-1　English Speaker 2

文学作品における病気というのは、単なる病気の描写ではなく、現代の社会が抱える問題の比喩であることが多いのです。例えば、1947年のアルベール・カミュ、1995年のジョゼ・サラマーゴ、2018年のリンマといった作家は、疫病を比喩として使っています。急速な感染拡大や、抑圧的な集団思考の危険性を表現しました。それは、つまり自立的な批判的思考の欠如を意味しています。他にも、ヴァージニア・ウルフが1925年に、医療危機の中で生きる人々の感情的、精神的な試練について焦点を当てて扱っています。パンデミックについての文学、これはただ単に病気の描写ではないのです。

-2　Japanese Speaker 1

In Japan, also, "La Peste" by Camus became a bestseller. This work, published in 1947, is a novel that likens the Nazis – in the War that ended two years before – to a plague; it gives thorough consideration to questions such as how people fall into chaos when society is attacked by great forces that go beyond human capabilities, and how those forces may be opposed. In this novel many people die; but there are also those who take action to save the lives of the sick, and it may be that Camus was entreating us not to forget those memories but to pass them on to the next generation.

-3　Japanese Speaker 2

Feeling the influence of the current coronavirus crisis, Japan's literary magazines have been putting together special editions in their latest issues one after another, publishing features about novels that use societies where infection is spreading as their setting. A main theme of these novels is healthcare workers, delivery drivers, supermarket cashiers, and people who are trapped in straitened financial circumstances. Hereafter we will find ourselves in an age which will call into question how we come to grips with the trauma of those people who have experienced particularly bitter situations. At that time literature and the field of the Arts, which cultivate humans' empathetic powers, can be expected to play a more important role than hitherto.

●-4　English Speaker 3

物語によって、病気というものの性格が形づけられます。医療危機における作家たちの傾向の一つとして病気を病理化することが挙げられます。つまり病気を誰かのせいにするということがよくあります。例えば、新型コロナウイルスが「中国ウイルス」と呼ばれるように、ドストエフスキーは『罪と罰』の中で、ロシアを襲った謎の病気を「アジア熱」と呼びました。また、イタリア・ルネッサンスの詩人であるジローラモ・フラカストロは梅毒を「フランス病」と定義しました。過去の文学作品を見返してみると、人間は危機に際して一致団結することに問題を抱えていたようです。

●-5　Japanese Speaker 3

In the novel "La Peste", one of the characters, a doctor named Rieux, has a scene in which he says the following to a young newspaper reporter, Rambert: "There's no question of heroism in all this. It's a matter of common decency. That's an idea which may make some people smile, but the only means of fighting a plague is – common decency." Rambert, upon hearing this, asks what he means by 'common decency', to which Rieux replies: "I don't know what it means for other people. But it my case I know that it consists in doing my job." This message is an important hint given to all of us trying to live in a post-corona world.

あとがき
「橋の架からないところに、橋を架ける」

柴原　智幸
（同時通訳デモンストレーション担当ゲスト）

　禅の世界に「不立文字」という言葉があります。本来は悟りに関する言葉なのですが、私は「本当に大事なことは、言葉に出来ないものである」という一般的な意味でとらえ、通訳や翻訳をする際に常に念頭に置いています。

　AIによる自動通訳・翻訳技術が発達した今、単純に「ザックリと意味を知る」だけなら、機械に任せることが一般的になりつつあります。そんな時代だからこそ、通訳を学ぶことの重要性がますます高まっていると、私は思います。

　通訳を学ぶとは、単純なやりとりではない、繊細なコミュニケーションに意識を集中させ、コミュニケーションの最高到達点を押し上げていくことだからです。逆を言えば、「やはりこれは機械には任せられない」という高レベルのコミュニケーションに焦点をあてて意識していくこと、コミュニケーションの本質をあぶりだすことでもあります。

　英日の通訳においては、「このスピーカーは日本語を話せないが、もし話せたとしたら、どんな言葉を選んで、どんな語り口で聴衆にメッセージを届けるだろう」ということまで想定して通訳を行います。自分がスピーカーに成り代わって、「表現しなおす」のです。

　この「表現しなおす」という行為において特に、「不立文字」の考えが生きてきます。通訳をする際には、言語メッセージ（言葉によるメッセージ）だけではなく、非言語メッセージ（表情やジェスチャーなど、言葉によらないメッセージ）も重要だからです。例えば、同じ「元気だよ」という言葉も、ガッツポーズをとりながら言うのと、微笑を浮かべて眉毛をハの字にしながら言うのとは、意味合いが全く違ってきます。

　さらに言えば、相手の言葉は、相手が「伝えたい」と思っていることを十全に言い表せていないかもしれません。それでも、こちらとしては「行間を読む」ような形で、全力でスピーカーのメッセージをくみ取りに行く。そして、こちらのクライアントの細やかな心の動きを相手に伝える際も、常に「これでもまだ表現し足りないかもしれない」という意識を持って、最善の上にも最善を尽くすわけです。

　言葉が異なる2者の間には、本来は十分なコミュニケーションは成立しません。通訳という行為は、そこを何とか成立させようとすることに、大きな価値があると思います。言葉にならないことを、言葉にしていく。橋の架からないところに、橋を架けていく行為なのです。

柴原　智幸 / Shibahara, Tomoyuki
神田外語大学専任講師。上智大学外国語学部英語学科、英国・バース大学大学院通訳翻訳コース卒業。帰国後は、ディスカバリーチャンネルの映像翻訳（吹き替え）を行い、2003年から現在までNHKで放送通訳者・映像翻訳者として勤務。2011年4月より2017年3月までNHKラジオ講座「攻略！英語リスニング」講師。

TOPIC 1 (2018)
English script writer : Michelle Henault Morrone
Japanese script writer : Kaoru Yoshimi

TOPIC 2 (2019)
English script writer : Lucy Glasspool
Japanese script writer : Kaoru Yoshimi

TOPIC 3 (2020)
English script writer : Lucy Glasspool
Japanese script writer : Kaoru Yoshimi

通訳ワークブック　著者情報

浅野輝子　　名古屋外国語大学名誉教授。学生通訳コンテストコーディネーター。
　　　　　　名古屋地方裁判所、高等裁判所法廷通訳人。「あいち医療通訳システム」推進
　　　　　　協議会副会長。医療通訳養成講座専門家委員。

吉見かおる　名古屋外国語大学　現代国際学部・現代英語学科准教授。
　　　　　　専門分野：多文化共生、移民・難民研究、日系アメリカ人史

グラスプール・ルーシー（Lucy Glasspool）
　　　　　　名古屋外国語大学　現代国際学部・現代英語学科准教授。
　　　　　　専門分野：ジェンダー論、セクシュアリティ、ポップカルチャー、ファンカ
　　　　　　ルチャー

ミッシェル・エノー・モローネ（Michelle Henault Morrone）
　　　　　　名古屋学芸大学　ヒューマンケア学部　子どもケア学科兼大学院　子ども
　　　　　　ケア研究科教授。
　　　　　　専門分野：比較教育学

花村加奈子　コミュニティ通訳者。主に愛知県警察、名古屋地方検察庁にて通訳に従事。
　　　　　　名古屋外国語大学非常勤講師。

キーワードで「現代」を伝える

通訳ワークブック2
NUFS英語教育シリーズ

2022年8月31日　初版 第1刷発行

編　著　　浅野 輝子　吉見 かおる
　　　　　グラスプール・ルーシー
　　　　　ミッシェル・エノー・モローネ

発行者　　亀山郁夫
発行所　　名古屋外国語大学出版会
　　　　　470-0197　愛知県日進市岩崎町竹ノ山57番地
　　　　　電話　0561-74-1111（代表）
　　　　　https://nufs-up.jp

音声録音協力　森 幸長

本文デザイン・組版・印刷・製本　株式会社荒川印刷

ISBN 978-4-908523-38-0